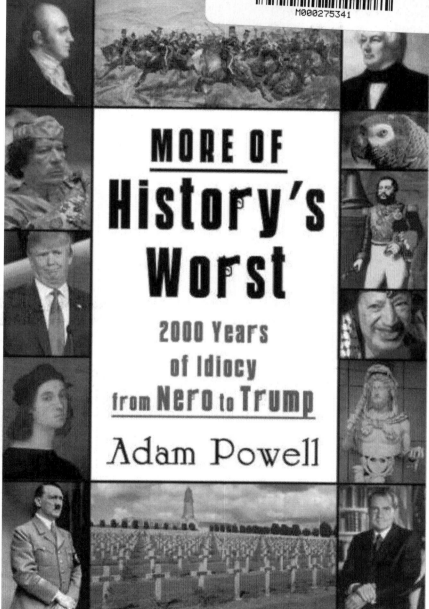

MORE OF
History's
Worst

2000 Years
of Idiocy
from Nero to Trump

Adam Powell

Robert D. Reed Publishers * Bandon, OR

Robert D. Reed Publishers
P.O. Box 1992
Bandon, OR 97411
Phone: 541-347-9882; Fax: -9883
E-mail: 4bobreed@msn.com
Website: www.rdrpublishers.com

Editor/Designer/Cover: Cleone Reed

Soft Cover ISBN: 978-1-944297-66-4

EBook ISBN: 978-1-944297-67-1

Library of Congress Control Number: 2020938051

Designed and Formatted in the United States of America

Dedication

To my wife Carmen, who makes everything possible.

"Adam Powell once again rewrites history with this inspired comic collection of frauds and fanatics."

~ **Brian Huggett,**
editor of *People of Few Words Anthology*

Contents

Introduction

"Two things are infinite: the universe and human stupidity;
and I'm not sure about the universe."
~ Albert Einstein

If there's a theme to this book it can be summed up by Douglas Adams. "It is a well-known fact that those people who must *want* to rule people are, ipso facto, those least suited to do it... anyone who is capable of getting themselves made President should on no account be allowed to do the job." There are exceptions of course, but for every Lincoln there are a dozen Warren Hardings. Monarchs, chosen by genetic lottery, don't seek power—they're just corrupted by it. Even Nero made a decent start to his reign before descending into megalomania.

History's Worst was written in response to the many "best of" collections. I've always found failure a far more interesting topic. From the king who thought he was made of glass to the dictator turned voodoo god—idiocy provides us with an endless source of comedy.

PART ONE:

Mad, Bad, and

Dangerous to Know

Uneasy Heads: History's Maddest Monarchs

"Uneasy lies the head that wears a crown."
~ **William Shakespeare, King Lear**

Why has madness been such an occupational hazard for royalty? Inbreeding doesn't help; some of them were so genetically challenged they might have auditioned for *Deliverance*. Then there were the pressures of the job. Imagine being constantly watched for twenty-four hours a day. Is it any wonder so many lost it?

1. George III of Great Britain (r. 1760–1820)

George seems to have been a normal child with no sign of any mental abnormalities. He was a slow learner but that was hardly unusual for the British Royal family. In fact, in his early reign, he was possibly the most boring monarch in Europe. No hobby was too tedious for George, and he was at his happiest discussing farming techniques or his model ship collection.

His first attack of madness came on in 1788, and he suffered from reoccurring bouts for the rest of his life. Doctors now believe the cause to be porphyria—a rare, hereditary disease that has affected members of his family, though never with such severity.

During his attacks, George's moods swung from deeply gloomy to ecstatically manic. He imagined London was drowning or spoke to people long since dead. He mistook a tree in Hyde Park for the King of Prussia. Public engagements became sources of embarrassment or amusement, depending on your attitude to the monarchy. George once started an address with the words, "My Lords and Peacocks."

At the end of his life, George cut a pathetic figure, wandering around his apartments without purpose, unbuttoning and buttoning his jacket, and talking nonsense to anyone who'd listen.

2. Charles II of Spain (r. 1665–1700)

"I am bewitched and I well believe it;
such are the things I experience and suffer."
~ Charles II

The Habsburgs always swam in the shallow end of the gene pool. First cousins got hitched; uncles wed nieces. Prospective brides were sized up at family reunions, resulting in a history of mental and physical abnormalities. Charles' father, Philip IV, continued the long Habsburg tradition of keeping it close by marrying his niece. This might explain poor Charles II. Deformed and imbecilic, even by Habsburg standards, he found talking and writing intellectually challenging. His jaw was so misshapen he couldn't eat solid foods.

Hoping to continue the family line, they arranged a marriage with a French royal. The marriage proved childless and she took to overeating, eventually gorging herself to death.

Charles' end came in 1700. Not yet forty, but already senile, he brought Habsburg rule to a close in Spain.

3. Maria I of Portugal (r. 1777–1816)

"Queen Maria, fancying herself damned for all eternity,
therefore on the strength of its being all over for her,
eats barley and oyster stew Fridays and Saturdays
and indulges in conversations of a rather unchaste nature."
~ William Beckford

Lunacy frequently knocked on the door of the Portuguese royal family and strangest of all was Maria I. She became obsessed after the deaths of her husband (also her uncle), two of her children, and her confessor in quick succession.

Maria was convinced she was going to hell and attended mass several times a day. She suffered from severe melancholy and terrible nightmares. She could often be found running around the corridor crying "Ai Jesus!" According to the writer William Beckford, she saw images of her dead father, "in colour black and horrible, erected on a pedestal of molten iron, which a crowd of ghastly phantoms were dragging down."

In 1807, the royal family fled to Brazil after Napoleon's invasion. This did little to ease her troubled mind. Some native dancers turned out to welcome her in traditional costumes, but Maria believed she had finally arrived in hell and was being attacked by demons. After that, they confined her to a convent until her death.

4. Frederick William I of Prussia (r. 1640–1688)

"The most beautiful girl or woman in the world
would be a matter of indifference to me,
but tall soldiers— they are my weakness."
~ Frederick William I

Frederick William I was a highly effective, if cruel, ruler, but his weird and obsessive behaviour qualifies him for this list. His ambition was to make Prussia a first-rate European power. To do this, he wanted Prussians to be as hardworking, frugal and disciplined as he was. He would walk around Berlin with a stick, beating anyone who was slacking or rip the clothes off women who were expensively dressed. He was so miserly he made the Queen wash up.

His moods grew darker with age. He was sometimes seized by terrible depressions when he would sit alone and cry or he'd lash out at anyone for the slightest mistake. His son Fritz was made to grovel publicly on the floor and kiss his father's boots.

Frederick William's one extravagance was his army. He built up a huge force, taking particular pleasure in recruiting tall soldiers. He named them his "blue boys" because of their bright uniforms and would kidnap youths over a certain height. Frederick William was so fond of his giants, he refused to deploy them in battle in case they were killed. He preferred to march them around his bedroom.

As soon as Fritz inherited the throne he sent the blue boys off to war

5. Ferdinand I of Austria (r. 1835–1848)

Once more into the Habsburg gene puddle. Few have been as nutty as Ferdinand I who combined madness with extreme stupidity, and had an abnormally large head along with the Habsburg's famous jaw.

This harmless halfwit's favourite hobby was jamming himself into a wastepaper basket and rolling around the room. Ferdinand would have made an excellent village idiot had he not inherited the Austrian crown. His father's deathbed advice was "don't change anything." The power of Ferdinand's intellect can be gathered by some of his remarks. "I am Emperor—I want dumplings, so give me them" and, "It is easy to govern, but what is difficult is to sign one's own name." On hearing that the people were having a revolution in 1848, Ferdinand's response was to ask, "Are they allowed to do that?"

Shortly afterwards they asked him to step down from the Austrian throne. He readily agreed.

6. Christian VII of Denmark (r. 1766–1784)

"I am confused, there is a noise in my head."
~ Christian VII

As a boy, Christian already showed signs of being disturbed. He would foam at the mouth and roll on the floor after being chastised. He'd wander around Copenhagen, "enjoying his freedom" as he described it. This consisted of boozing, brothels, and beating up strangers. There might have been a touch of overcompensation as he was short and puny.

He didn't improve when he became king. He liked to leapfrog over people when they bowed, or suddenly slap courtiers on the cheek. Often whole apartments in his palace were smashed, leaving room after room empty of furniture. As the years passed, Christian's moods became more unpredictable. No one was safe from attack. He suffered from delusions that he was about to be assassinated or he was really the son of Catherine the Great.

He unofficially stepped aside when his son reached sixteen, much to the relief of the court, but Danes could still see their ruler making faces at them from his apartment window.

7. Emperor Norton I of the United States and Protector of Mexico (r. 1859–1880)

He never ruled the United States of course. He was a gentle loon living in San Francisco, but in his own mind he was very much the man in charge. Emperor Norton took his governmental responsibilities seriously, publishing state proclamations in the local newspapers. He corresponded with Abraham Lincoln and Queen Victoria. By 1860 he became so worried about the nation he called for a convention to right the country's wrongs. Sadly, no member of Congress attended. Nine years later he tried to abolish the Democratic and Republican Parties to encourage national unity.

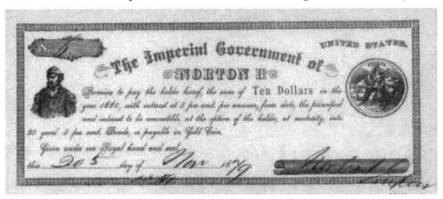

Norton built up quite a following over the years. Mark Twain wrote him a poem after the emperor's beloved dog died. When he was once arrested and placed in an asylum, there was such a public outcry that the chief of police had to apologize. Norton was immediately released. After that, all San Francisco policemen started saluting him in the street.

When Norton died, more than twenty thousand attended his funeral. Many saner men have been less mourned.

8. Don Carlos of Spain (b. 1545–d. 1568)

Back to the Habsburgs, this time the Spanish branch. Don Carlos was the heir to a vast domain, which stretched from Spain to South America. But his behaviour became so impossible his father Philip II had him imprisoned*.

As a child, he enjoyed torturing servants and animals. He bit the heads off snakes and testicles off of dogs or incinerated rabbits. In adulthood, he bullied servants and counsellors at the slightest provocation. Don Carlos once made a cobbler eat a pair of shoes that didn't come up to scratch. Food, as well as cruelty, was a passion and he ballooned.

Frustrated by having no political role, *His Porkiness* schemed to break up his father's empire and rule the Netherlands. He may have even plotted to kill Philip. When his father discovered this, Don Carlos was arrested and locked in a tower. Hopes that he would eat himself to death failed to materialize (though not from a lack of effort: in one sitting Don Carlos stuffed down a salted pie big enough for eight people) so poison was applied. Exit Don Carlos to general applause.

* For the usual Habsburg reason, interbreeding had left him with six great grandparents instead of the usual sixteen.

9. Charles VI of France (r. 1380–1422)

Until 1392 he was a likeable youth without a hint of the insanity, but while out riding one day he suddenly attacked and killed five of his men. His mental state never recovered. He started believing he was made of glass and that iron rods were holding up his body. His treatments could hardly have helped. They included boring a hole through his skull or having his servants dress as demons and leap out to scare him back to sanity.

His daughter's marriage to Henry V of England might have been responsible for some later English regal eccentricities.

10. Ludwig II of Bavaria (r. 1863–1886)

"I wish to remain an eternal enigma to myself and to others."
~ **Ludwig II**

Ludwig's attempt to make Bavaria into a major European power was a hopeless failure. He then retreated from the real world into a fantasy existence, building fairy-tale castles that almost bankrupted his country. He also enjoyed rowing in a seashell-shaped boat inside his private grotto while a lackey read poetry to him. His frolics with young soldiers and actors did not endear him to the conservative Bavarian court. Placed under house arrest, Loopy Ludwig later drowned in mysterious circumstances, swimming with his psychiatrist.

Cruel Rule: History's Nastiest Royals

The line between madness and cruelty is often blurred and some on this list were clearly strangers to reason. They are here because they were more sadistic than lunatic.

1. Genghis Khan, Founder of the Mongol Empire (r. 1206 –1227)

"The greatest happiness is to vanquish your enemies... to rob them of their wealth and see those dear to them bathed in tears, to clasp to your bosom their wives and daughters."
~ **Genghis Khan**

Using a combination of cruelty and cunning, Genghis Khan led his Mongol hordes to conquer the biggest land empire the world has ever known. Fuelled by yaks' milk and horses' blood, these sophisticates burnt, raped, and looted their way from China to Poland. Cities that didn't immediately surrender were razed to the ground, their inhabitants slaughtered.

The conquest of Northern China compares with the Nazi invasion of Russia in its brutality. Whole areas were turned into "hunting parks" and depopulated. Some parts of the Hsi Hsia region took centuries to recover. As one scholar wrote, "It was the most extensive devastation and wholesale slaughter which China had known."

2. Ivan IV "the Terrible" of Russia (r. 1547–1584)

Old Ivan killed folks here and there
And murdered his own son and heir
But most think the Tsar
Went that bit too far
By using the skin of a bear
~ **Mick Twister**

Ivan had a miserable childhood. He was orphaned young and suffered neglect and mistreatment from a series of noblemen. He would take out his anger on animals by throwing them from towers or pulling off their legs.

When he was seventeen, he established absolute rule in a wave of violence against his tormentors. Tsar Ivan had some early successes, but the death of his first wife hit him hard and he became indifferent to the suffering of others. His acts of savagery defy the imagination. He would rape women and then have them buried alive, drown beggars or use them for target practice. When he suspected the inhabitants of Novgorod of being disloyal, he massacred most of its population. The city's archbishop was dressed in a bearskin and hunted by a pack of dogs.

Ivan formed a secret police force called the "Oprichniks" who terrorized much of the country in random orgies of violence. Ivan would organize parties for them where the main entertainments were drinking and torture. Those close to him also suffered. His seventh wife was drowned because Ivan discovered she wasn't a virgin. One loyal servant was boiled alive. He murdered his eldest son during an argument though he later showed genuine remorse.

By the time he died, there were few families in Russia that hadn't suffered in some way from his rages.

3. Leopold II, King of Belgium (r. 1865–1909)

"I was so moved, Your Excellency, by the people's stories that I took the liberty of promising them that in future you will only kill them for crimes they commit."
~ John Harris, Missionary in Baringa

"I have undertaken the work in Congo in the interest of civilisation and for the good of Belgium."
~ Leopold II

Leopold II was King of Belgium, one of the most democratic states

IN THE RUBBER COILS.

in Europe. But being the figurehead of a tiny European country was not enough for him. He dreamed of a vast empire. Leopold's plans for colonisation met with little enthusiasm at home, so he organised a private company, the International African Society. This was to be a private colony, not subject to the will of the Belgium parliament. The army, the Force Publique, answered directly to him.

The resource rich Congo looked ideal. He sent troops to "protect" the native Congolese from Arab slavers, but this was a smokescreen. Leopold wanted to get his hands on the Congo's lucrative rubber and ivory. He told one of his representatives, "I do not want to risk... losing a fine chance for ourselves a slice of this magnificent African cake." Eventually, the "Congo Free State" would be seventy times the size of Belgium.

Even by the awful standards of European behaviour in Africa, the occupation marked a new low. Not until the Nazi Holocaust were atrocities carried out on such a scale against a defenceless people. Estimates vary but perhaps ten million people died from cruelty and European diseases. Villages were burnt at random. They cut the hands off Africans if they didn't meet their rubber quota. Bonuses were paid on the amount of hands collected. They figured it saved money on bullets.

Eventually, after an international outcry (the brutality inspired Joseph Conrad's *Heart of Darkness*) Leopold reluctantly agreed to cede direct control to Parliament but his legacy continues to this day. The Congo remains one of the most violent, traumatised places on earth.

4. Vlad the Impaler of Wallachia
(r. 1448, 1456–62, 1476)

The legend of Dracula is loosely based on this vicious monster, though he makes Bram Stoker's fictional *Prince of Darkness* seem positively benign.

His nickname derives from his favourite method of killing people. Impalement was a slow and agonizing death, where a spike slowly pierced the victim. It could take days to die. Vlad enjoyed watching the executions with his meal. Men, women and children, nobles and peasants— it didn't matter.

20

He killed as many as one hundred thousand people in his short reign, including twenty thousand Turkish prisoners of war in what became known as the "Forest of the Impaled." Vlad also had people boiled alive, flayed, or pushed off cliffs onto spikes. He once ordered the turbans of two Muslim diplomats to be nailed to their heads when they refused to remove them in his presence. People were executed for the most trivial reasons: minor theft, lying, cheating—one woman was killed because her husband's shirt was the wrong length.

Romanians still honor him though because he stood up to the Hungarians and Turks.

5. Peter the Great Tsar of Russia (r. 1685–1720)

Historians have often praised Peter as the great modernising Tsar of Russia, but they tend to gloss over just how much his people suffered as a result. An example is the building of his glittering new capital, St Petersburg, which cost the lives of thousands of serfs, worked to death in its construction. It was one of the greatest acts of forced labor in history.

Peter wanted to drag Russia out of its backwardness and become a more advanced "western" country. He wouldn't tolerate anyone in his way. He executed his son Alexis for not being enthusiastic about his reforms. A physical bully (he was six foot eight) and a despot, Peter personally took part in the torture of army officers who plotted rebellion. He hated anything to do with "Old Russia," like the traditional beards men wore. He would shave or tear out the facial hair of those around him.

By the end of his reign, Russia had become a great power, but the serfs were the most downtrodden in Europe.

6. Murad IV of Turkey (r. 1623–1640)

"The wine is such a devil that I have to protect my people from it by drinking all of it."
~ **Murad IV**

In Murad's mercifully short reign, thousands were killed at his behest. No offence was too trivial for execution. Smoking, drinking alcohol and coffee were all punishable by death. The sultan also murdered anyone who annoyed him. He impaled a courier who

mistakenly said Murad's new child was a boy rather than a girl. Those who sang too loudly, had fat necks, or walked too near his palace were executed. He seems to have derived a sinister pleasure in drowning women.

This scourge of alcohol died at 27 from kidney failure, brought on by too much drinking.

7. Queen Ranavalona I of Madagascar (r. 1828–61)

She prevented Madagascar falling under colonial rule but her ruthlessness reduced the population by half. Her power rested on control of the army who subjected people to periods of brutal forced labor. One notorious example was during a buffalo hunt, she wanted a road built immediately for herself and her retinue. Ten thousand died during its construction. She dispensed justice by the tangena test. Poison was extracted from the nut of the tangena and fed to the accused. If you died then you were guilty; if you lived then you didn't do it.

8. Kaiser William II of Germany (r. 1888–1918)

For his huge role in starting World War I, William II deserves a place on this list. "Kaiser Bill" pursued a reckless foreign policy, antagonising former friends like Britain and Russia into joining an anti-German alliance. Perhaps his aggressive behaviour can be explained by his sense of inferiority caused by a withered arm.

William was an anti-Semitic bigot to boot.

Whatever the reasons, the war he did so much to cause cost the lives of over nine million people.

9. Nader Shah of Persia (r. 1736–1747)

Nader Shah was a brilliant military commander, who was as cavalier with the lives of his subjects as he was with his enemies. He tortured and murdered Persians at random, sometimes making towers out of their heads. He even blinded his son. Eventually, his commanders, fearful for their own lives, had him murdered.

10. Queen Nzinga of Angola (1583–1663; r. early 17th century)

As sexually active as she was cruel, she had a harem of lovers who were made to fight gladiatorial battles to the death. The winner got to sleep with the Queen. Then he was killed.

Nzinga also executed women if they became pregnant.

Power Corrupts:
History's Most Insane Modern Dictators

*"Power tends to corrupt but absolute power tends to corrupt
absolutely"*
~ Lord Acton

1. Adolf Hitler, Germany and lots of other places
(ruled 1933 –1945)

*"Hitler reminds one so much of someone in a psychiatric
hospital who says 'I own the banks; I own the businesses; I'm
the most powerful man in the world.' But the most frightening
thing was that he was. He made his fantasies become reality."*
~ Dr Anthony Storr, Psychiatrist

Some dictators became insane after years of wielding power. Surrounded by sycophants and drunk with their own importance, they gradually lost touch with reality. Hitler on the other hand was always possessed by demons. Even as a dropout in Vienna or a soldier in the First World War, he was never a regular guy. It was madness that propelled him to power, not power that drove him to madness.

Hitler only ever cared about two people: his mother and his niece (and possible lover) Geli

Raubal. After Geli died, Herman Goering thought Hitler lost any trace of human sympathy. Certainly, in World War II he was as indifferent to the sufferings of Germans as he was to his enemies.

Tales of his abnormal behaviour are well publicized, but surely anyone who chewed carpets when annoyed needed a decent anger management course. Perhaps the most pathetic aspect of Hitler was his flights from reality when the going got tough. The Soviets were bombarding his bunker in 1945, yet he still found time to design fantasy cities. As if the Soviets were going to let him work as an architect after the war.

= 1. Pol Pot, Cambodia (ruled 1975–1979)

"What is rotten must be removed."
~ a Khmer Rouge slogan

"Whether you live or die is not of great significance."
~ Pol Pot

Was Pol Pot insane? He seemed more rational than Hitler, though admittedly that's a low hurdle. He came across as less egotistical than Mao or Kim Il-sung. There was no extreme personality cult in Communist Cambodia. In fact, Pol Pot hated mass gatherings and was shy among strangers. Yet if a complete indifference to the sufferings of others is a form madness, this quiet, withdrawn man definitely qualifies. During his four years as leader, almost a quarter of Cambodians were killed. Think about it: NEARLY TWENTY-FIVE PERCENT shot, starved or brutalized in a terror regime that outstrips Stalin, Mao, and Hitler, when population size is considered.

Pol Pot remained unrepentant after his eventual arrest. "Our movement made mistakes" he graciously conceded, but asked, "Am I a savage person? My conscience is clear."

Pol Pot seized power after President Nixon's bombing campaign rendered the country ungovernable. The US dropped more bombs on Cambodia than on Japan during World War II. The Khmer Rouge, Pol Pot's fanatical supporters, then tried the most radical communist experiment in history, taking their cue from Maoist China but with steroids. Mao's Great Leap Forward was the worst manmade disaster in human history, yet this didn't put off Pol Pot launching a "Super Great Leap Forward." Even the ailing Mao told Pol Pot to tone down the extreme behaviour of the Khmer Rouge.

When Pol Pot entered the capital, Phnom Penh, his enemies were dispatched with alacrity. Teachers, doctors, the religious, civil servants, people whose hands were soft (therefore clearly of bourgeois stock) were shot. Those too young, old or sick to work met a similar fate. The "lucky ones" were forced out of urban areas to help create Pol Pot's rural socialist utopia. Cambodians worked from four in the morning to ten at night, in what became known as the Killing Fields. You had to subsist on one tin of rice every two days, doing backbreaking manual work. Many died of starvation or diseases related to malnutrition.

Cambodia effectively became one large concentration camp. No offense was too petty: you could be shot for eating a piece of fruit you had picked, talking unnecessarily or even laughing; it was serious work building an agrarian socialist utopia.

For the Khmer Rouge, life was not so hard. They feasted on special food, enjoyed imported luxuries and went to China for medical treatment.

Communism is theoretically about equality, but Pol Pot's regime was deeply xenophobic and targeted racial minorities. Vietnamese, Chinese, and Cham Muslims were shot on mass: about half the Chinese population in Cambodia died during these years. Pol Pot also hated the family, which he thought a relic of the old regime. Young children were removed from their parents and indoctrinated in huge communal schools that resembled barracks. Young adults were forced to marry spouses that were selected by the party. This did not apply to Pol Pot who divorced and chose his second wife. Their daughter didn't go to one of those barracks.

Life was utterly miserable for ordinary people. TV, religion, holidays, radios, music, and newspapers were banned, and bicycles confiscated. Foreign products were forbidden, unless you were a senior party member. There was only a single shop in the whole of Cambodia; not that it mattered as you couldn't buy anything— money had been abolished. The economy plummeted, of course, testing the loyalties of even the most diehard of his followers. When Vietnam invaded after border tensions, Pol Pot started a vicious purge of anyone he thought disloyal, including some of his closest supporters. It was too late. Many joined the Vietnamese forces and Pol Pot fled, bringing the four-year nightmare to an end.

Even today, Cambodia is still a traumatized nation. One wonderful book to read is Frances T. Pilch's *Invisible: Surviving the Cambodian Genocide, The Memoirs of Mac and Simone Leng*. It's a very human story about what it was like living in Cambodia under Pol Pot's dictatorship.

Skulls from the stupa memorial at the killing fields of Choeung Ek, near Phnom Penh, Cambodia. © Brad Barnes, 2007

The most graphic reminders of the Khmer Rouge are the skulls and bones still displayed in the Killing Fields, testament to the brutality of this quiet, withdrawn man.

2. Nicolae Ceausescu, Romania (ruled 1965–1990)

"One of the great leaders of the world."
~ **Richard Nixon**

Nixon's praise for this loathsome bully was typical. Western leaders queued up to honour Ceausescu, because of his willingness to criticize the Russians. During the Cold War, any enemy of the Soviet Union was guaranteed a warm reception in the free world.

What they ignored was that Ceausescu was probably the nastiest, and nuttiest, dictator in post-war Europe—no mean feat considering the competition. The self-styled "Genius of the Carpathians" reduced one of the most fertile countries in the world to near starvation. They exported agricultural products to pay off Romania's debts, while the only meat regularly available to Romanians were pigs trotters—nicknamed "patriots" as they were the one thing that never left the country.

Ceausescu dealt with repression mercilessly: they put political opponents in lunatic asylums where they were made to build their own coffins. The real loonies were busy running the country. In this paranoid world, typewriters were banned. Romania under Ceausescu became a mix of Stalinism and Alice in Wonderland. Bibles sent by missionaries were pulped and used for toilet roll, but the job was done so badly that Romanians could still read words like "God" and "Jesus" when relieving themselves after their delicious patriots. The "Genius of the Carpathians" once had a giant hole in a building site filled in and a park created overnight, just so he could make a speech there. Afterwards, the park was destroyed and the hole dug again.

Ceausescu and his charming wife Elena became increasingly paranoid as the years rolled by. They had their clothes disinfected every day to prevent them from being poisoned. For the same reason, Ceausescu always washed after shaking hands, even when they met the Queen of England. They brought their bed linen on trips abroad.

Not everyone was treated badly under Ceausescu. He took a liking to a dog named Corbu, who was given the rank of colonel in the Romanian army. Corbu had his limousine, television, phone, and personal food taster. The Ambassador to the UK had to go shopping in London for his favourite dog food. But some animals were more equal than others.

When they caught a parrot saying "stupid Nicu" he was arrested and interrogated. Nicu was Ceausescu's son, so obviously some subversive plot was afoot. The parrot was later throttled and buried in a secret grave.

3. Kim Il-sung, Korea (ruled 1948–1994)

Kim Il-sung's personality cult made Mao's seem positively humble. "The Eternal Great Leader" was credited with the usual totalitarian blather about helping peasants with their crops and building steel works with his bare teeth. But he also possessed supernatural powers, as the following anecdote from the North Korean press demonstrates:

"One day... two white magpies perched on a branch of a pine tree in the garden as president Kim Il-sung was working. It (sic) was rare to be seen in Korea in more than five hundred years. When an official came out with a movie camera, the two birds flew away. The president told him that they would surely fly back again. In the afternoon two days after, the magpies flew in the gardens as he predicted. They were photographed so that all the people of the country might see them."

Out of gratitude for feats like this, each citizen carried a badge with Kim's picture. And if anyone hadn't had enough of his image, there were large posters of him on all public buildings. In Pyongyang, one lane of each street was reserved for his personal use. As no one else owned a car, this didn't matter.

Dictators often proclaim themselves "President for Life" after they've consolidated their regimes. Kim went one better by becoming "President for Death." So important was he for North Korea's future development, when he died Kim still retained the title of president while his son took over as general secretary.

Kim Il-sung's death was clearly a tragedy for North Korea. When the "Not-so-Eternal Great Leader" croaked in 1994, the North Korean media reported that animals cried at the news. The fact that he was still running the country from the grave wasn't enough to cheer them up.

4. Ne Win, Burma (ruled 1962–1988)

Many heads of state have been superstitious. But there's one thing putting on a lucky tie-clip before a big speech, quite another letting superstition take over your government.

Ne Win is a case in point. His erratic rule of Burma was often due to consulting astrologers, numerologists, and soothsayers—then basing policy decisions on whatever they told him. In 1970, people had to switch from driving on the left to the right because a soothsayer had told Ne the country was too left wing. When he heard his lucky number was nine, he introduced a new currency with dominations of forty-five and ninety as they were divisible by nine. For those who had savings in the old currency, it was a Ne Win situation (sorry about that). He also announced he would live to ninety. He was hardly rational in his private life either, bathing in

31

dolphin's blood to keep him young and walking backwards over bridges to escape harmful spirits.

He died at age ninety-one, so the fortune-tellers were crap after all.

5. Colonel Gaddafi, Libya (ruled 1969–2011)

"...a sort of Austin Powers of international politics"
~ **Bridget Kendall**

Gaddafi was an irritant to the Western world for over forty years, funding some nasty terrorist groups in his time. This didn't stop Libya holding the Chair of the United Nations Human Rights Commission, which must have impressed the families of Pan Am Flight 103.

He loved throwing Libya's money away, literally. Gaddafi once had the idea of creating a single African super state, and selflessly offered his services as leader. A number of African rulers cannily invited him to their country for discussions, providing he splashed the cash.

In his 2002 trip to Malawi he threw six million dollars into the crowd. Needless to say, there was a great turn out.

Gaddafi had psychiatric treatment but it made no difference. BBC journalist John Simpson said interviewing him was a genuinely strange experience. Gaddafi would answer by "throwing back his head and laughing long and loudly at the roof of the tent," even if the questions were of a serious nature. Simpson once saw Gaddafi turn up at a press conference arranged for the Libyan leader. After walking through the crowd of journalists smiling and waving, he quickly exited before answering a single question.

He always claimed to be true to his Bedouin roots by living in a tent. However, when he travelled he lived more like the aging rock star he came to resemble. On foreign trips he'd take a personal jet, a couple of transport aircraft, a container ship, a few buses, his own personal hospital, and enough food for a regiment. It was as if Pink Floyd were on tour again. To complete the picture of 1970s decadence, he employed heavily made-up female bodyguards. What they made of that in Malawi is anyone's guess.

6. Idi Amin, Uganda (ruled 1971–1979)

"(Amin) is a bit thick... a little short of the grey matter."
~ **A British army officer shortly before Ugandan independence**

"A splendid type and a good (rugby) player... but... virtually bone from the neck up, and needs things explained in words of one syllable.
~ **A British Official**

The assessments are unfair; Amin was not as stupid as his oafish demeanour suggested. What he was, though, was a sociopath, killing up to half a million people in eight blood-soaked years.

When he came to power after a military coup, he had a lot of international support. Amin professed a love for the Scottish way of life and had a penchant for kilts and bagpipes. For many, this amiable clown seemed preferable to the lefty intellectual, Milton Obote, who had just been kicked out of office. Amin's willingness to mug for the cameras made him seem harmless to the outside world, and some of his anti-European jokes struck a chord with fellow Africans. Amin had himself carried in a litter by white businessmen, and once offered food aid to Britain during an economic crisis there. He asked the Queen to come to Uganda to get to know "a real man," and then awarded himself the Victoria Cross and the Crown of Scotland.

But Ugandans saw Amin's other side. His purges were savage in the extreme. Amin seemed to have enjoyed the whole process. He kept one political opponent's head in his refrigerator. He'd sometimes stomp on his victims, feed them to crocodiles, or order political prisoners to club each other to death.

Amin turned one of Africa's most prosperous countries into an economic basket case by expelling Uganda's seventy thousand Asians who made up most of its business community.

As time went on he became even odder. Amin started professing an admiration for Adolf Hitler (unusual for an African) and placed a statue of the Fuhrer in Kuala Lumpur. He declared war on Tanzania and offered to fight Julius Nyerere, its respected leader, in the boxing ring. The Tanzanians were unimpressed and invaded Uganda, forcing Amin out of power.

7. Jean-Bedel Bokassa, Central African Republic (ruled 1966 –1979)

"(Bokassa) earned the reputation of, at best, a buffoon, and at worst of a blood-thirsty killer."
~ Julian Nundy

The Cold War was a wonderful time to be dictator. Providing you got Western or Soviet protection, you could murder your subjects with impunity. Jean-Bedel Bokassa is a fine example of an unhinged despot who enjoyed the support of the French government for years.

Bokassa came to power in a military coup in 1966 and established the usual tyranny. He brutalized the people into submission whilst robbing the country of its wealth. He crowned himself Emperor of the Central African Empire in a ceremony that cost forty million dollars (bankrolled by the French), despite the fact that the economy had collapsed. He then proceeded to strut under the title of Bokassa I. He was referred to as "Apostle," but after meeting Colonel Gaddafi he announced his conversion to Islam, changing his name to Salah Eddine Ahmed Bokassa. How his seventeen wives and fifty-five children fitted in with either Christianity or Islam was never explained.

When a group of children protested about the cost of school uniforms, Bokassa had over a hundred imprisoned, tortured, and murdered, taking an active role in the proceedings. Rumours that he ate some of them have never gone away, and he was later charged with cannibalism as well as murder.

The more the French found out about his regime, the more hostile they were to their government's support of Bokassa. He had given France a steady supply of uranium for its nuclear power stations, while a gift of diamonds to President Giscard d'Estaing probably ensured the Frenchman's defeat at the subsequent election. After the news of what had happened to the schoolchildren became known, d'Estaing supported an invasion of the Central African Republic that ended Bokassa's rule.

Exile followed and then prison; the frail Bokassa was released in 1993. A journalist interviewed him a year later. Dressed in white robes (he was now a Catholic), he claimed to be appointed by the Pope for some special Christian duties. Bitter to the end, Bokassa felt let down by his old pals. Not only had he won World War II single-handedly but they also hadn't thanked him for the diamonds. "I fought for France;" he said, "I liberated France from the Nazis. I called Giscard my cousin. And they betrayed me."

8. Saparmurat Niyazov 'Turkmenbashi', Turkmenistan (ruled 1990 –2006)

"If I was a worker and my president gave me all the things they have here in Turkmenistan, I would not only paint his picture, I would have his picture on my shoulder, or on my clothing..."
~ **Saparmurat Niyazov Turkmenbashi**

"I'm personally against seeing my pictures and statues in the streets...but it's what the people want."
~ **Saparmurat Niyazov Turkmenbashi**

If anyone thought the collapse of communism would bring an end to despotic fruitcakes, they were swiftly disappointed. Exhibit A is Saparmurat Niyazov Turkmenbashi, the egotist who misruled Turkmenistan for over a decade. Turkmenbashi, an old Communist Party hack, transformed himself into an ardent nationalist when the Soviet Union disintegrated. Turkmenistan had huge gas reserves and a population of only five million, but his lavish building projects and gross incompetence made it the poorest nation in the region.

In Absurdistan every whim became law. Turkmenbashi banned opera, lip-synching, make up for male television presenters, car radios, beards, and long hair. Drivers had to pass a morality test to get a license. He ordered citizens to extract their gold teeth and recommended chewing chicken bones after meals. Every second Sunday in August became "Melon Day" to celebrate the nutritional properties of the "Turkmenbashi melons." Given the state of dental hygiene, they probably couldn't eat much else.

"The Father of all Turkmen" brought the personality cult to a new level. The nation's capital, a meteorite, January, and the main port were all called... Turkmenbashi. His image appeared on vodka bottles, the currency, and classroom walls; a gold-plated statue of "His Excellency" graced the skyline of Turkmenbashi, rotating 360 degrees so it always faced the sun. But Turkmenbashi couldn't have created this paradise by himself. He modestly acknowledged the second most important person in Turkmenistan's history—his mother, naming April and the national loaf after her.

While pensions were stopped and hospitals closed, the grandiose projects just kept rolling along. There was the man-made lake in the desert, a giant pyramid, an ice palace, and, in the land of the disappearing journalist, an enormous book-shaped building called the House of Free Creativity to celebrate freedom of speech. Considering the level of censorship, it was like King Herod building a monument to childcare.

Turkmenbashi fancied himself as a bit of a philosopher and his musings were collected in *The Book of the Soul*, which became

compulsory reading in schools, universities, and for those important moral driving tests. He insisted on regularly reading it out loud on television or reciting some of his poetry. So wonderful was his verse that it won the national poetry competetion. Main judge? Who do you think?

Turkmenbashi died suddenly in mysterious circumstances. Since his death, much of the silliness has been done away with, but thankfully Melon Day still remains.

9. Dr. Jose Gaspar Rodriguez Francia, Paraguay (ruled 1814–1840)

Jose Francia, nicknamed El Supremo, was a puritanical maniac who turned Paraguay into the most isolated country in Latin America. All contact with the outside world ceased, while foreign visitors were imprisoned for years.

Overseas trade was stopped and immigrants were forced to do unpaid labor. Nobody was allowed to leave.

Francia modeled himself on his hero, Maximilian Robespierre, and like that humourless fanatic he hated people having fun—frivolities such as newspapers and fiestas were banned. El Supremo became so suspicious of everyone around him he rebuilt Asuncion in a grid formation, so conspirators would be easier to spot. He dressed all in black to instill fear, a century before Mussolini. He had a particular dislike of the institution of marriage and had seven illegitimate children, encouraging Paraguayans to do the same.

All in all, Francia made Paraguay one of the most boring places on Earth, but he was very good at balancing the state budget, a Latin American first.

10. Francois "Papa Doc" Duvalier, Haiti (ruled 1957–1971)

"God and the people are the source of my power.
I have twice been given power.
I have taken it, and damn it, I will keep it."
~ **Francois "Papa Doc" Duvalier**

Dictators usually think themselves above the mass of humanity, but few have been egocentric enough to believe they were divine. Francois "Papa Doc' Duvalier had no such qualms.

He dressed as Baron Samedi, the voodoo spirit of the dead, wearing a top hat, tuxedo, and sunglasses. Papa Doc (he was a real doctor and thought he was a father to the illiterate peasantry) deliberately spoke in a nasal voice like Baron Samedi and named his secret police the Tonton Macoute, after a mythic creature who disappeared people forever—a common enough fate in Haiti. Duvalier also exploited Catholicism by putting Jesus Christ and himself on the same poster, Jesus resting his hand on Duvalier saying the words, "I have chosen him."

His deranged behaviour has been explained by a serious heart attack when he was deprived of adequate oxygen for over eight hours. However, the cause might have been hereditary as his mother suffered from mental instability.

Haiti was terrorized for over a decade, while the public finances were raided by Duvalier and his cronies. Businessmen and professionals fled if they could, and Haiti became the poorest country in the Western Hemisphere. The weird and frightening atmosphere of the time is captured in Graham Greene's novel *The Comedians*.

Papa Doc's death in 1971 left the country in the hands of his oafish son Jean-Claude 'Baby Doc" Duvalier who subjected Haitians to a further fifteen years of misery.

Old School: Sociopaths of the Ancient World

"I have no faith in human perfectibility. I think that human exertion will have no appreciable effect upon humanity. Man is now only more active—not more happy—nor more wise, than he was 6000 years ago."
~ Edgar Allen Poe

1. Nero, Roman Emperor (r. 54–68 ACE)

Nero's childhood was a traumatic one. Many of his relatives were killed by the Emperor Tiberius, and he experienced poverty and exile under Caligula. His father Gnaeus was a heartless bully who once ran over a child for a joke. Gnaeus died when Nero was four, and he was brought up by Agrippina, his domineering mother. Agrippina became obsessed with Nero's advancement. His squinty eyes and body odour didn't help her plans—Nero could fell a centurion at a hundred paces— so Ma married Emperor Claudius and persuaded him to make Nero his heir. Once Claudius agreed, he was poisoned and Nero became Emperor at just eighteen years-old.

After a decent beginning, the excess and executions started. Absolute power went to the head of this already unbalanced man. He designed a collapsible ship to drown his mother. When she escaped he had her captured and murdered. Nero killed two of his three wives, kicking one of them in the stomach while pregnant. He poisoned his potential rival, Britannicus.

Nero loved to write poetry so audiences were locked into the theatre and had to sit through hours of his doggerel, and then wildly applaud at the end. Hopefully, they weren't sitting downwind.

Squinty is infamous for fiddling while Rome burned in 64 ACE. This never happened. Nor did he start the fire that ravaged the capital. What contributed to his unpopularity was the attention he gave his new palace, a massive structure that took twenty percent of Central Rome. Many Roman's didn't relish their tax money going on this folly while their own homes lay in rubble. Nero callously blamed the fire on Christians, and they were herded into the amphitheatre to be eaten by lions or used as human torches for his parties.

Soon the Roman elite called time. A plot to kill the Emperor was hatched but discovered, and Nero had the ringleaders put to death — including the philosopher Seneca. Feeling secure, he went to Greece to perform in an arts festival; naturally he won first prize in every event. But trouble was brewing back home. After his return, the Senate declared Nero an outlaw and ordered him to be flogged to death. Rather than face his enemies, Nero had himself stabbed in the neck.

His last words were, "What an artist dies with me."

2. Caligula, Roman Emperor (r. 12–41 ACE)

"There was never a better slave or a worst master as Caligula."
~ Tiberius

"Caligula is best understood as an infant allowed to be infinitely terrible by an obsequious Senate and subject to no restraint or authority."
~ Anthony Blond

Perhaps his horrible upbringing contributed to his behaviour: his father, mother, and brothers were all murdered. Possibly it was genetic: his family included such villains as Tiberius and Nero. Whatever the reason, Caligula has become a byword for depravity.

Where do you start? Caligula might not have made his horse a consul, but he slept with three of his sisters. He also debauched the

42

wives and daughters of other Romans and then gave detailed accounts of his conquests. He forced his chamberlain to commit suicide after cuckolding him. Sensitive about his hair loss, Caligula executed people for looking down on his skull. Baldy once had some audience at a Roman game fed to the wild animals for a laugh. He would whip people personally if they talked during a performance of his favourite actor. Despite his own private life, Caligula could be a prude: he burned a playwright just for writing a crude joke.

Caligula's egotism reached epic proportions when he proclaimed himself a god and demanded to be treated as a deity. When someone once hesitated to answer who was greater, Caligula or Jupiter, the man was beaten to death. Fortunately for Rome, his tyranny ended when the Praetorians stabbed him outside a theatre. They were the guards who protected Caligula, but they figured it was Rome that needed protection.

3. Nabonidus, King of Babylon (r. 556–539 BCE)

Nabonidus' mind seriously declined towards the end of his reign. He believed he was a goat and enjoyed crawling on all fours, eating grass.

4. Locusta of Gaul, Professional Poisoner Date of birth unknown–c.68 ACE)

She was the greatest poisoner of all time. The Emperor Claudius was her most famous victim, as was his son Britannicus. Under Nero's protection, she opened up a school for poisoners with an impressive alumnus. Locusta and her students killed over ten thousand people, mostly for rich nobles and Nero. An early experimenter in empirical sciences, she kept a stable of slaves to try out her potions. When Nero was deposed she was executed.

5. Vitellius, Roman Emperor (r. 69 ACE)

"Being besides a man of an appetite that was not only boundless but also regardless of time or decency, he could never refrain, even when sacrificing or making a journey, from snatching bits of meat and cakes amid the altars, almost from the very fire, and devouring them on the spot; and in the cookshops along the road, viands smoking hot or even those left over from the day before and partly consumed."
~ Suetonius

This glutton ruled Rome briefly in 69 ACE, in a reign characterized by extravagance. He advanced his career by shamelessly sucking up to Nero and being a gambling buddy of Claudius, but his big break came when he was promoted to Governor of Lower Germany by the Emperor Galba. Galba thought such a mediocrity would never be a danger, but Vitellius' troops encouraged him to march on Rome. On the way his forces defeated the new emperor Otho. When Vitellius visited the battlefield (he had stayed away during the fighting) he remarked, "Only one thing smells sweeter to me than a dead enemy and that is a dead fellow citizen." Vitellius then shocked Romans by not giving Otho and his supporters the proper Roman burial rites. It was a taste of things to come.

Taste being the operative word with Vitellius. He would put away four feasts a day; in one of them two thousand fish and seven thousand birds were consumed. They described him as having a "vast belly"—no kidding. The only thing he enjoyed as much as scoffing was killing. In a few months he dispatched astrologers, diviners, people he owed money to, old friends, a man who asked for a drink of water (Vitellius gave him a glass of poison instead), and his mother.

Soon soldiers flocked to Vespasian, the competent governor of Judea, as a rival candidate. When Vespasian approached Rome, most of Vitellius' troops went over to the other side. Vitellius realized he'd lost and disguised himself as a janitor, but they soon discovered him cowering in a room with furniture propped against the door. After some gratuitous torture, Bigbellius was executed. Only the chefs mourned.

6. Attila the Hun, Ruler of the Hunnic Empire (r. 434–453 ACE)

"The barbarian nation of the Huns, which was in Thrace, became so great that more than a hundred cities were captured and Constantinople almost came into danger and most men fled from it... And there were so many murders and blood-lettings that they could not number the dead. Ay, for they took captive the churches and monasteries and slew the monks and maidens in great numbers."
~ **Callinicus, in his Life of Saint Hypatius**

Attila the Hun is now being reappraised by historians. No longer the barbaric killer, they see him as a strong, unifying leader. This would have been a surprise to the thousands of people he slaughtered, raped, and tortured. (He sometimes had his opponents literally torn apart.) Maybe he had issues. Not only did Attila murder his brother, but he encouraged his wife to feed him a pie of baked sons. Brings a whole new meaning to family dinners.

7. Qin Shi Huang, Chinese Emperor (r. 220–210 BCE)

He unified China; he brought us those terracotta soldiers; he built much of the Great Wall—and was a thoroughly nasty piece of work. Under Qin Shi Huang, laws were so harsh they make Draco look like a bleeding-heart liberal. They overtaxed peasants to the point of starvation. He burned priceless works of Chinese literature if they did not conform to his narrow view of the world, and four hundred and sixty of China's best scholars were buried alive.

The terracotta army, marvellous though they are, were to protect him from angry gods in the afterlife. And the brilliant men who carved these sculptures? Killed, so no one would know the secret of their construction.

8. Elagabalus, Roman Emperor (r. 218–222 ACE)

"Finally, he set aside a room in the palace and there committed his indecencies, always standing nude at the door of the room, as the harlots do, and shaking the curtain which hung from gold rings, while in a soft and melting voice he solicited the passers-by."
~ Cassius Dio

They put him on the throne by his mother and grandmother in a convoluted plot. Elagabalus was only fourteen years old. His odd religion and boundary-pushing sexual practices (and that's saying something in ancient Rome) led to his assassination.

According to accounts, he asked a doctor to give him a sex change and had all his body hair plucked. While he was emperor, he enjoyed pretending to be a prostitute in the taverns of Rome. This did not prevent him marrying five times during his reign, once to a Vestal

Virgin, once executing a former husband shortly before the marriage.

Elagabalus was an obsessive worshiper of the El-Gabal, a black stone he transported around. He made it the official deity of Rome. This cult included the sacrifice of sheep, cattle, and human genitals, and the encouragement of temple prostitution. All this didn't endear him to Romans, perfectly happy with their own whacko religions. They were particularly annoyed that their tax money went on a great temple to the holy boulder. Elagabalus then married it to the statue of Minerva when he wed the Vestal Virgin. There was rarely a dull moment in Imperial Rome.

9. Polycrates, Tyrant of Samos (r. 538–522 BCE)

A Greek tyrant, he terrorized the Aegean world until power eventually went to his head. Polycrates took control in Samos by killing one brother and exiling another. At the beginning of his reign he was tough but capable, and a fearsome commander. He plundered many Greek islands and cities, defeating Lesbos and Miletus.

Then came the inevitable hubris. Polycrates' friend Amasis, King of Egypt, advised him to try a little hardship in his life by sacrificing something. The gods after all do not take kindly to humans who are too happy. So Polycrates took his prized emerald ring and flung it in the sea. Later a fisherman brought him a fish as a present and, when it was cooked, they found the ring in the fish's stomach. Polycrates now thought himself blessed by the gods. According to Herodotus, he became increasingly erratic. He teamed up with the Persians to topple his old friend Amasis. Polycrates had his fleet manned by misfits and criminals and planned to have them killed, but they saw what was in the air and joined the Egyptian side. In Samos he destroyed the gymnasia to end gay relationships but kept a male lover, Smerdis. He then cut off Smerdis' hair when a poet admired his looks.

It was greed that finally did it for Polycrates. Herodotus said he was always "very fond of money" and was tricked into visiting the Governor of Sardis, Oroetes, when he sent Polycrates a chest crammed with rocks. The governor had the top layer of the chest covered with gold coins, guessing it would lure Polycrates to Sardis. The tyrant's daughter begged him not to go. She had a nightmare about her father being killed while lifted into the air. Eager for loot, Polycrates ignored her advice and visited Sardis. When he arrived Oroetes had him crucified.

10. Commodus, Roman Emperor (r. 180 –192 ACE)

"Yet Commodus was not, as he has been represented, a tiger born with an insatiate thirst of human blood, and capable, from his infancy, of the most inhuman actions. Nature had formed him of a weak rather than a wicked disposition. His simplicity and timidity rendered him the slave of his attendants, who gradually corrupted his mind. His cruelty, which at first obeyed the dictates of others, degenerated into habit, and at length became the ruling passion of his soul."
~ Edward Gibbon

In Gladiator, Commodus is the psychotic emperor with a love for gladiatorial contests. Though most of the movie is inaccurate, it got that part right. Commodus obsessed about being a gladiator while the Empire went to pot.

After foiling an assassination plot in 182 ACE, he became delusional. Officials were executed or their children were kept as hostages. He holed himself up in his villa and started developing his combat skills. He announced he would put on, and star in, gladiator games. This was ridiculous; gladiators were on the lowest rung of Roman society. It would be like the US President taking part in WWE (World Wrestling Entertainment).

Ironically his father, Marcus Aurelius, had hated these sports but Commodus revelled in them. His warm-up event was animal massacring. During one festival he killed a hundred bears and ostriches, lopping the heads of the birds with a bow and arrow (okay, he was a good shot). This sickened the Roman crowds. They particularly objected when he killed a giraffe—the best gladiators were admired for their bravery, not butchery.

Next came human combat, and in every event the Emperor always won. Not a surprise when his opponents were armed with wooden swords (Commodus' was metal). In public he would rarely kill his opponent, but in private contests it was a different matter. He sliced off ears or noses to show his skill as a swordsman. Commodus had a statue made boasting he had killed ten thousand men. For each performance he charged an appearance fee of one million sesterces; this exorbitant sum emptied the city coffers.

His rampant egotism reminded people of Caligula rather than his quietly spoken father (and there were rumours that he was the son of a gladiator, not Marcus Aurelius). When Central Rome was rebuilt after a fire, he wanted to rename it the Colony of Commodus; the army legions would be called the Commodianae. The months of the year would be named after him—luckily he had twelve names.

Commodus developed an obsession with Hercules. He dressed in a lion skin and commissioned sculptures of himself in Herculean poses. In imitation of his hero's giant slaying, the historian Cassius Dio wrote, "...he got together all the men in the city who had lost their feet as the result of disease or some accident, and then, after fastening about their knees some likeness of serpents' bodies, and giving them sponges to throw instead of stones, killed them with blows of a club, pretending they were giants."

By 192, ACE, a group of senators decided he had to go. First, one of his mistresses tried to poison him but he vomited it up. Then, in a fitting death, Commodus was strangled... by one of his gladiators.

PART TWO:
Incompetence beyond the Call of Duty

Executive Stress: History's Worst Presidents

No one has been selected because of his political views. Corruption, incompetence, or "wrong man, wrong time" are the main qualifications. As the list shows, no party has a monopoly on incompetence. But the defunct Whig Party deserves a special mention. They only produced four presidents, yet three have made this list. An impressive seventy-five percent idiocy rate. We have missed them.

1. Warren Harding (Republican, 1920–1923)

"He has a bungalow mind."
~ **Woodrow Wilson on Warren Harding**

"I am not fit for this office and never should have been here."
~ **Warren Harding**

A joke at the time went, "What's the difference between George Washington and Warren Harding?" "Washington cannot tell a lie; Harding cannot tell a liar." It sums up the most naïve man ever to become president. This gullible buffoon appointed a bunch of crooks to government jobs who lined their pockets at the public's expense.

Most notorious was Albert B. Fall, Secretary of State for the Interior. Fall's job was to protect the environment, but it was the environment that needed protecting from Fall. His biggest scam was the Teapot Dome scandal, where he illegally leased naval oil reserves to private business for kickbacks. Then there was Colonel Forbes, an ex-army deserter, who organised the theft of two hundred million dollars intended to help war veterans. Even the Attorney General got in on the act and had to resign over accusations of selling liquor permits and pardons. Old progressives must have looked on in horror at the graft and growth of trusts. It was the Gilded Age all over again.

Publicly, Harding supported a return to family values, but behind closed doors, it was golf, gambling, and girls. He even earmarked a closet near the Oval Office where he could entertain his mistress. The partying president was also partial to a drink when prohibition was in force.

Harding had a talent for mangling the English language that became legendary. E. E. Cummings wrote, "The only man, woman, or child who wrote a simple declarative sentence with seven grammatical errors is dead." H. L. Mencken was even more vitriolic, "Warren Harding is the master of a language in which the relations between word and meaning have long since escaped him. Harding's style reminds me of a string of wet sponges; it reminds me of tattered washing on the wall... of stale bean soup, of college yells, of dogs barking idiotically through endless nights. It is so bad that a grandeur creeps into it."

For those who think the modern media is too intrusive in public lives, Warren Harding is the case for the defence. He physically looked like presidential timber, but all those around him knew he wasn't up to the job. They kept the public in the dark during his presidency. Millions mourned when they learned that Harding had died from a probable heart attack. If people had known what was going on, there would have been a collective sigh of relief.

2. James Buchanan (Democrat, 1857–1861)

"My dear sir, if you are as happy on entering the White House as I on leaving, you are a very happy man indeed."
~ **James Buchanan to Abraham Lincoln**

So low had Buchanan's reputation sunk after his presidency, his portrait was removed from the Capitol Rotunda to stop it being defaced. It was America's misfortune that such a man presided over the nation's affairs on the eve of the Civil War.

Buchanan thought the best way to heal divisions between North and South was to give slaveholders everything they wanted. He encouraged the spread of slavery into Kansas and the Territories, and favoured the strict enforcement of the Fugitive Slave Act—the "Bloodhound Bill"—that allowed slaveholders to pursue their "property" across the country. Buchanan believed the abolition of slavery would result in the "introduction of evils infinitely greater..."

which meant freed African-Americans would start to massacre their "chivalrous" former masters. Buchanan showed a similar sympathy for the plight of the poor.

During his presidential campaign he announced that ten cents a day would be enough for a workingman to live on, earning him the nickname of "Ten-cent Jimmy." He left office for a comfortable retirement on more than ten cents a day, while America was engulfed in the Civil War he had helped start. Buchanan died believing history would exonerate him. He was wrong.

3. Franklin Pierce (Democratic President 1853–1857)

"Here lies the body of my good horse... for twenty years he bore me around... in all that time he never made a blunder. Would that his master could say the same."
~ **Franklin Pierce**

While America tore itself apart over states' rights and slavery, Pierce had a struggle of his own. He was often the loser of a well-fought bottle. Befuddling his way through a disastrous term, the nation slid towards conflict as Pierce drunkenly slid under the White House tables.

What the country needed was leadership at a time of crisis; what they got was a strict constructionist who thought the president's role was to do as little as possible.

Cometh the hour, cometh the pedant.

4. Richard Nixon (Republican President 1969–1974)

"(Nixon's) one of the few in the history of this country to run for high office talking out of both sides of his mouth at the same time and lying out of both sides."
~ **Harry Truman**

"If I had my time again, I would like to have ended up a sportswriter."
~ **Richard Nixon**

Even with the expletives deleted, Nixon's time in office makes grim reading. C.R.E.E.P., executive privilege, the Saturday Night Massacre, tape tampering. Watergate resembled a Shakespearean tragedy where a brilliant man is brought low by personal flaws.

Yes, he did some good things: Détente with Russia, ping pong with China. But Kissinger was wrong when he said people would forget Watergate and remember the achievements. At least not yet. Forget the annoying habit of putting "gate' after every minor scandal. This diminishes the magnitude of Nixon's sins. No one has ever besmirched the office of president as much Nixon, and for that he is on the list.

And we haven't even mentioned the bombing of Cambodia.

5. John Tyler (Whig 1840 –1844)

"Tippecanoe and Tyler too."
~ **Whig campaign slogan. Tippecanoe was Harrison's most famous battle and his nickname.**

"Poor Tippecanoe! It was an evil hour that Tyler too was added to make out the line. There was rhyme but no reason to it." A Whig delegate after John Tyler had been chosen for the vice-presidential nomination.

It seemed like a good idea at the time. Put up a vice presidential candidate from a different section with different political views and maximize your vote. Why worry? No president had ever died in office. So ran Whig thinking when they asked John Tyler to run with the old warhorse, William Henry Harrison. Only when the aging general succumbed to pneumonia four weeks into his term did the full horror of what they'd done dawn on them. Tyler wasn't meant to be president! Tyler was really a Democrat. He'd only left his former party over a tiff with Andrew Jackson and was against everything the Whigs were for.

They tried numerous schemes to strip him of his powers, like proposing all the cabinet should have an equal vote on every issue. They wanted to call him Acting President, but Tyler refused to answer any correspondence with that title. One Washington wit suggested The Executive Ass would be more suitable. Then they tried impeachment. Not enough votes. Congress even refused to pay for Tyler's heating expenses. At one point the whole cabinet resigned except Daniel Webster who was out of the country.

Tyler has the dubious distinction of being the only president to have been buried without state honours. This is because he broke his constitutional oath by sitting in the Confederate House of Representatives.

6. Millard Fillmore (Whig 1850–1853)

"God Save us from Whig Vice Presidents."
~ **Northern Whig saying inspired by Fillmore**

Fillmore did little in office and what he did was usually wrong. A man who put party before country, his main achievement was signing the Great Compromise of 1850.

He was America's second accidental president and, like Tyler, was never intended for the top job. Even though Fillmore recognized slavery as morally evil, he thought pacifying slaveholders was the best way to keep the Whig Party together. It wasn't. The Compromise of 1850 merely delayed the Civil War. Within it was one of the most hateful pieces of legislation in US history, the Fugitive Slave Law (see James Buchanan) which so angered Northern Whigs they stopped Fillmore's nomination for a second term. Later he ran for president as the candidate for the openly racist Know-Nothing Party. He carried one state.

A Society for the Preservation and Enhancement of the Recognition of Millard Fillmore was later formed, "Dedicated to the celebration of mediocrity in American culture... " Dave Barry lists Fillmore's greatest achievement as "The Earth did not crash into the Sun" during his presidency.

7. Martin Van Buren (Democrat 1837–1841)

"As to the Presidency, the two happiest days of my life were those of my entrance upon the office and my surrender of it."
~ **Martin Van Buren**

Van Buren could "cry out of one side of his face and laugh out of another."
~ *Davy Crockett*

In 1837 President Andrew Jackson was so popular he could have chosen his dog to succeed him. He picked the equally dutiful Martin van Buren. It was an excellent choice, if craftiness and cunning were the prime qualities for a president.

Such was Van Buren's trickiness he was nicknamed the Little Magician by his enemies. It was even rumoured he was the illegitimate son of Aaron Burr, the "crooked gun" who had been Jefferson's vice president. He certainly resembled Burr, who had regularly stayed at the inn where Van Buren was born. Both men shared a talent for intrigue.

Van Buren had started his career in New York's sleazy Tammany Hall politics but advanced by attaching his lips firmly to Andrew Jackson's ass. No amount of flattery was too gross. He once called Jackson the greatest man in history behind his back knowing this would reach the president. When Jackson heard what Van Buren had said he wept. Van Buren cleverly managed to alienate Jackson from other potential successors; at one point he even persuaded the entire cabinet to resign.

Van Buren's problems began when he finally made it to the Oval Office. Like most kiss-ups, he was more capable of following orders than giving them and proved unable to deal with the economic recession. To cries of "Martin Van Ruin" he was trounced at the next election.

8. Andrew Johnson (Unionist 1865–1869)

"This is a country for white men, and by God, as long as I am President, it shall be a government for white men."
~ **Andrew Johnson.**

"And to think that one frail life stands between this insolent, clownish creature and the presidency! May God bless and spare Abraham Lincoln."
~ **The New York Times.**

There are things to admire about Andrew Johnson. His childhood made Lincoln's seem privileged. Brought up in a cabin smaller than a prairie outhouse, he could not even afford to go to school. He taught him-self to read and trained as a tailor.

Gradually he rose through the Democratic Party, showing a rare concern for the lives of the poor—providing they were white. When the Confederacy was formed he was the only dissenting southern sena-tor, braving lynch mobs and threats of assassin-nation. Lincoln respected his guts and asked him to be his running mate for the 1864 election. Then the curse of the balanced ticket set in. After Lincoln's assassination, Republicans found themselves having to work with a states' rights Democrat who opposed any attempt to help former slaves. Johnson proved so inflexible he alienated even the most moderate Republican. While the Ku Klux Klan ran rampant and former Confederates were imposing the Black Codes, Johnson tried to veto the Freedman's Bureau, the Fourteenth Amendment' and the Civil Rights Act. As historian Jay Cottle wrote: "(Johnson) revealed political ineptitude and an astonishing indifference toward the plight of the newly freed African-Americans."

9. Herbert Hoover (Republican President 1929–1933)

"We are nearer today to the ideal of the abolition of poverty and fear from the lives of men and women than ever before in any land."
~ **Herbert Hoover one year before the Great Depression**

"(Hoover is) the perfect self-seeker... His principles are so vague that even his intimates seen unable to put them into words... He knows who his masters are, and he will serve them."
~ **H.L. Mencken**

Hoover was an energetic and talented man who had done wonders organizing famine relief in Belgium and Russia. In another era he would have been a good president. But he was unable to deal effectively with the Great Depression which simply overwhelmed his administration.

Hoover seemed not to grasp the scale of the crisis that hit America after the Wall Street Crash. When unemployment reached twenty-three per cent, he refused to give direct aid, believing it would sap people's will to find work, even though work was a fast disappearing commodity. After finding out that some Americans were peddling fruit on street corners, he remarked, "Many people have left their jobs for the more profitable one selling apples."

In order to create a sense of "business as usual," he ordered no change to White House ceremonies. Seven-course meals were still served by immaculately dressed flunkeys. It must have cheered those waiting in soup kitchen lines to know their president was living like Louis XIV. Not that they had much to complain about. According to Hoover, "Nobody is actually starving. The hobos, for example, are better fed than they have ever been. One hobo in New York got ten meals in one day."

One of Hoover's last acts was to send troops against desperate World War One veterans who came to Washington to ask for the payment of their war bonuses. For many this showed the heartlessness of a man once known as a great humanitarian.

Hoover has had a whole lexicon of phrases named after him. Hoovervilles were shanty towns for the destitute that sprung up during the Great Depression. A Hoover Flag was an empty pocket turned inside out. A Hoover Blanket was a cover made from old newspapers.

10. William Henry Harrison (Whig 1841)

"Old Tip he wears a homespun suit,
He has no ruffled shirt, wirt, wirt;
But Matt he has the golden plate,
And he's a little squirt, wirt, wirt."

It may seem unfair to nominate someone who served for only four weeks, but Harrison is on the list for running the shallowest campaign in electoral history, for choosing John Tyler as his vice president, and for dying in office. Letting John Tyler serve almost a full term is unforgivable.

In 1840 the Whig Party thought they were in with a chance of the presidency. The country was mired in recession and President Martin Van Buren was getting most of the blame. They treated the public to the first modern election where spin and jingles replaced tedious stuff like issues. Above is one of the more cerebral ditties. Matt was the incumbent Martin Van Buren who they accused of having a privileged background. Unlike their man who was born in a log cabin and liked nothing better than to swill cider when not ploughing his fields. In reality, Harrison was from the Virginia aristocracy whose humble cabin was an eighteen-room mansion. This didn't stop the Whigs coming up with efforts like,

"Let Van from his cooler of silver drink wine
And lounge on his cushioned settee;
Our man on his buckeye bench can recline
Content with hard cider is he!"

Harrison said nothing during the campaign in case he offended anyone, but once victorious he thought he'd make up for his silence. On a rainy November day, he delivered the longest ever inaugural speech: 8,420 words in all. Unfortunately, the elderly Harrison decided not to wear a hat and the resulting cold became pneumonia.

And so… 2016 came along and everything changed.

This book was originally about historical events. Monarchs and politicians had to finish serving their time in office before being considered. But so egregious has Trump's presidency been that he's earned a special guest slot.

President Donald Trump (Republican 2017–Present)

"I thought this would be easier." ~ **Donald Trump, after his first hundred days**

"To say Donald Trump would be a disaster for our country, our democracy, and our future would be doing a grave disservice to the word 'disaster.'" ~ **Tom Steyer**

He's not here because of his policies (they appeal to conservatives and anger liberals) but because of his behaviour. During the 2016 campaign, his antics would have sunk any previous candidate. He mocked the disabled and women he found unattractive, insulted racial minorities, demeaned Gold Star parents, and boasted of sexually assaulting women. Yet he won, with a little help from the Electoral College, but he won. Some hoped he would pivot to become more presidential. But three years on and we're still waiting. Truly a president without precedent.

Here's a summary of his more memorable moments.

Promoting the Trump family business interests while in office. This is prohibited by the Emoluments Clause in the Constitution but hasn't deterred the Donald; he ignored the advice of his ethics experts and didn't fully divest his assets. Trump has blurred the line between his family's business interests and his presidential duties. The appointment of his son-in-law, Jared Kushner, and daughter Ivanka, to senior advisory positions in the White House, despite their lack of experience, indicated how things would be. Letting Ivanka briefly sit in for him at G20 Summit of World Leaders (July 2017) showed how far he could go.

They often interviewed applicants for government posts at Trump Tower, not the White House, where the US military and security services pay handsomely to stay. Trump Hotels rented space to entities owned by foreign governments or for foreign embassies to host events. Barely a week after his inauguration, the initiation fees for his Mar-a-Lago beach resort doubled. Meanwhile Kellyanne Conway promoted Ivanka Trump's fashion brand on TV, an unusual interpretation of the presidential counsellor's role.

The Muslim ban included countries where not one national had ever launched an attack on the United States. Yet Saudi Arabia, Egypt and the United Arab Emirates weren't on the list—despite being where the 9/11 hijackers were actually from. Trump has done business with all these nations in the past.

The unprecedented use of taxpayers' dollars for private trips. Trump criticised President Obama for regularly golfing and promised not to play for three months in office. Within two weeks of becoming President, Trump was teeing off. The cost of these trips to US taxpayers has been roughly $130 million as of March 2020, vastly exceeding Obama. Others on Team Trump followed suit. Steven Mnuchin, the Treasury Secretary, spent over $800,000 of federal funds on seven military trips. Sadly, for Steve, his request for a government jet to take his new wife on their honeymoon was turned down.

Refusing to listen. Trump has a habit of ignoring inconvenient truths. The planet is facing an existential crisis as climate change that wreaks havoc. It is now the overwhelming scientific consensus that this is because of human interaction—but not with Trump. Somehow, he knows better. He dismissed it as a "hoax" invented by China, which he later falsely denied saying. He often confuses the weather and climate. What is becoming a regular is the president tweeting how we need some global warming whenever there's a bit of snow. Staff at the Department of Agriculture cannot use the terms "climate change" or "reduce greenhouse gases." The Energy Department's banned the phrases "Emissions Reduction" and "Paris Agreement."

Predictably, the environmental decisions of his administration have assumed that the natural world is there to be exploited rather than protected. Trump pulled out of the Paris Climate Agreement. The Clean Power Plan was replaced by the polluter-friendly Affordable Clean Energy rule. The Obama law that new cars should do at least fifty-four miles per gallon, was reduced to thirty-four. Rules governing methane emissions were relaxed, despite it being a major cause of global warming. National Monument land has been opened for mining and drilling. The Clean Water Act was rolled back, allowing for more chemical dumping in rivers and streams. In an effort to protect the coal industry, Trump let individual states decide whether to reduce carbon dioxide. Coal is dying; it employs five times fewer people than renewables, but Trump insists on boosting what he calls "clean coal," yet it's the dirtiest of all fossil fuels. Not content to wreck America's air, water, and soil, animals are also a target. Short-term economic gains have been prioritized over wildlife protection, as rules protecting endangered species were diluted.

This unwillingness to listen to others cost the US lives during the coronavirus pandemic. In Trump world he is right about everything; and no expert, no matter how qualified, no evidence, no matter how compelling, will dislodge this view. "This is just my hunch," he said, dismissing World Health Organisation figures about the spread of COVID-19. The US lost crucial time over Trump's subsequent inaction and misinformation, and by the end of April 2020, it had become the world's most infected country with over one million cases (more than ten times that of China).

Lying and rule-breaking. Don't all politicians lie? To an extent yes, like everybody else, but Donald Trump is in a league of his own. According to a *New York Times* survey, President Obama lied eighteen times in his eight years as president; Trump managed one-hundred and three times in the first ten months, or perhaps we should call them "alternative facts" as Kellyanne Conway does.

Here is a sample from his first ten days in office: Trump lied about the size of his inauguration crowd and the weather on the day; the number of people shot in Chicago while Obama was speaking there; the number of people shot in Philadelphia; the number of times he had been on the cover of *Time* magazine; Trump incorrectly said that new immigrants weren't vetted during Obama's presidency; he lied that the *New York Times* had apologized for its negative coverage of him; Trump denied that he had ever criticised the CIA over the Agency's claim that Russia had meddled in the 2016 Election; finally, he deliberately underplayed the number of people detained at US airports because of his travel ban.

And his presidency was less than a fortnight old.

For Trump, rules are like the truth, strictly for others. He has ignored the Constitution and bent laws more than Richard Nixon. He makes "Tricky Dicky" look like George Washington. The Mueller Report, for instance, did not exonerate him. It outlined, in forensic detail, ten cases where Trump attempted to obstruct justice, but there was doubt that they could prosecute a sitting president. What also came out of the Mueller Report was how hard those around Trump tried to prevent him from breaking the law, often ignoring his orders (fortunately, he's so unorganized he forgets what he tells staffers to do). Trump is staggeringly ignorant of the Constitution, but when he comes up against its checks and balances, he cannot accept the limitations of executive power. "Why can't I do that? I'm the President?" he frequently asks. He sees the presidential role as similar to running the Trump Plaza Casino: it's his so he can do what he wants.

This disregard for the rules isn't just confined to numero uno. The people around him often behave in a similar way–perhaps because of his influence, or maybe he just picks bad apples. A fair number of his associates have already been charged with criminal offences: Michael Flynn, Roger Stone, Michael Cohen, Paul Manafort, Konstantin Kilimnik, Rick Gates, and George Papadopoulos. How many more before his presidency ends?

Loyalty is more important than competency. Trump values loyalty above all else. "Is he loyal?" "Is she loyal?" was the refrain he constantly sang when deciding who to appoint. CVs weren't properly checked; social media was trawled to see if they had said anything bad about the Boss. This was an administration of neophytes. By September, twenty-two of Trump's appointments to the Department of Agriculture had no experience in agriculture; all of them had worked on his campaign. Former lobbyists were employed in departments they had lobbied against, violating ethical rules that Trump himself had approved. Sometimes candidates were actively hostile to the department or agency they now led. They put Scott Pruitt in charge of the Environmental Protection Agency, even though he had been a long-term critic when Oklahoma's Attorney General. Pruitt once tried to block the Clean Power Plan by suing the EPA. Pruitt's another climate change denier. During his tenure he rarely saw environmental groups but regularly met lobbyists for the oil industry, car manufacturing, and big agriculture. He was not a one-off. Betsy DeVos at Education, Rick Perry at Energy, and Ben Carson at Housing and Urban Development had previously been sceptical of the work their departments did. All happily shredded budgets and diluted functions. All are loyal to Trump.

But the granddaddy of unsuitable appointments was Michael Flynn as National Security Advisor. Trump had been warned by Obama, who'd fired him from the DIA, and by Chris Christie who headed his transition team. Both knew Flynn was wrong for such a key post. Flynn had been subject to a misconduct investigation when he was chief of Military Intelligence in Afghanistan and was being investigated by the security services over his Russian connections. Christie warned Trump, "He's going to get you in trouble." Trump sacked Christie instead. Why? Because, as Ivanka told Flynn when he was appointed, "Oh General Flynn, how loyal you've been to my father…" He even led the "Lock her up" Hillary chants at the Republican National Convention. Ironically, it would be Flynn who was charged with making false statements to the FBI about his Russian contacts. Trump didn't know all this, but he knew enough about Flynn never to appoint him.

Many have been forced out for simply doing their job and placing the rule of law and adherence to the Constitution above everything else. But that doesn't wash with Trump. Acting Attorney General Sally Yates was fired for refusing to implement the controversial Muslim ban, as she believed it contradicted the Immigration and Nationality Act. James Comey, the FBI head, is the standout case here. In a now-famous exchange in January 2017, Trump demanded "loyalty; I expect loyalty" from the boss of an independent agency. Trump later spelled out what this meant: letting Michael Flynn off the Russian charges. Comey's refusal to do so was partly a reason for his dismissal. He never forgave even an old friend like Jeff Sessions when he recused himself during Mueller investigation after two undisclosed meetings with the Russian ambassador. It didn't matter that he was the first Senator to endorse Trump. Sessions was then publicly undermined for months in speeches and tweets. Trump rarely fires people; he just makes their lives hell so they leave. This cruel streak is one of his least attractive features. Sending vicious tweets that would shame an eighth grader is well known. Less so was his treatment of members of staff like General H. R. McMaster, his second National Security Advisor.

Trump normally enjoys surrounding himself with military men (though not during the Vietnam War when it was his time to serve). They create the look he wants for his administration, just like the telegenic women he appoints. Trump, after all, comes from reality TV. He soon took against McMaster because of his habit of saying uncomfortable truths, rather than telling Trump what he wanted to hear. McMaster is everything Trump isn't. A distinguished war veteran and the author of a highly regarded academic study (unlike Trump, he writes his own books). He was scholarly, knowledgeable and gave detailed, objective advice about foreign policy. Trump does not do detail. One aide nicknames him the "two-minute man" because that's all you've got before he loses concentration. Trump started openly mocking McMaster, ignoring him in the middle of conversations or impersonating him when he walked into the room. He was fired by tweet like several others. It's that Trump mixture of cruelty and cowardice. Like all bullies, there is something of the coward in President Bone Spur. When face-to-face with a genuine threat, he tends to buckle. At the Helsinki Conference when standing next to Putin, he supported Vlad the Impaler's version that Russia didn't interfere in the 2016 election, rather than what his own security services were saying.

After three years in office, Trump has lost his best people: Jim Mattis, John Kelly, Gary Cohn, McMaster, Rex Tillerson—the adults in the room who thought they could tame Trump, make him more presidential. He is now surrounded by careerists, kiss-asses, ideologues, and family. Is it surprising so many terrible decisions are made?

His attitudes to race have been controversial. Despite his assertion that he is the least racist person that "you've ever encountered," Trump has sailed close to the wind with his racial stereotyping of African-Americans and Latinos. His behaviour has also revealed a disturbing attitude toward racial minorities. As far back as the 1970s, the Department of Justice sued Trump for refusing to rent to African-Americans. In the 1980s, when Trump and his then-wife Ivana went to his casino, they moved black employees off the floor. Trump denies this, but something similar happened a few years later when Trump was fined for moving African-Americans off gambling tables at the request of a customer. In 1989, Trump condemned the Central Park Five, a racially charged case where five black and Latino youths were accused of raping a white woman; Trump called for the death penalty in a newspaper advertisement. Later they were exonerated as their DNA didn't match and the real rapist confessed in prison. Trump, to this day, has refused to admit he wrongly condemned these men.

Another campaign with a distinctly racist tinge was the "birther" controversy. This was an attempt to delegitimize America's first black president with a fake story that Barack Obama was not born in the USA (and so should legally be excluded from his position). "Birtherism" started as a fringe conspiracy theory but was given a massive public boost by Trump's support with comments like, "He's spent millions of dollars trying to get away from this issue…And I'll tell you what; I brought it up, just routinely, and all of a sudden a lot of facts are emerging and I'm starting to wonder myself whether or not he was born in this country."

Trump's appointments also raised concerns among civil rights groups—people like Steve Bannon, who had a history of right-wing extremism, notably during his lengthy editorship of Breitbart, the website for the "alt-right" that peddled minority-baiting, Islamophobia, and fabricated scare stories about "black crime." None of this diminished him in Trump's eyes, and Bannon was made his campaign CEO and then Chief Strategist. Another white nationalist is Stephen Miller, one of Trump's senior policy advisors, who was a moving force behind the president's travel ban. Even after a leak of some of his emails, which showed him promoting extremist books and websites, Miller kept his job. Chief Scientist at Department of Agriculture Sam Clovis called progressives "race traitors."

Trump's actions have often matched his words. He ended federal funding for the "Life after Hate" program, designed to help young escapees from racist gangs. He pardoned Sherriff Joe Arpaio, a local Arizona law officer, who was found guilty of criminal contempt for continuing to target Latinos based on racial profiling, despite a court order. Trump described him as a "worthy candidate" for a pardon.

As part of his "zero tolerance" policy, children were separated from their parents when trying to cross America's southern border. The sight of children in wire mesh compartments stirred outrage at home and abroad, forcing Trump to issue an executive order stopping the measure, but family separations still continue albeit on a smaller scale. But Trump doesn't think all immigrants are bad—two of his three wives are from Eastern Europe. They can be thankful that Trump wasn't president when they wanted to move to the US.

Perhaps most troubling of all was President Trump's reaction to what happened in Charlottesville when a far-right rally and counter-protest ended in violence. A car was driven into a crowd of anti-racists; one woman was killed and nineteen injured. The demonstrators comprised Neo-Nazis, members of the KKK, and white supremacists chanting, "Jews will not replace us," yet Trump said there were "very fine people on both sides." Many Republicans condemned his response, like Orrin Hatch and Marco Rubio, but he delighted the extreme right. Former Ku Klux Klan Grand Wizard David Duke praised Trump for his "honesty." White supremacists believe Trump is softening up Americans to accept their point of view by making racism more respectable.

The promise to construct a wall, for example, was classic dog-whistle politics, designed to appeal to anti-Latino sentiment. It might energise his base but it's defective—like most of Trump's policies. The half-built fence—that Mexico never paid for—has cost almost thirty million dollars per mile. Part of it fell down in strong winds in January, 2020. By the end of 2019, less than a hundred miles had been constructed of the two thousand-mile border.

Many people who make the occasional verbal misstep aren't necessarily racist but such is the regularity of Trump's; it's reasonable to suggest this is more than the odd gaffe. Does Trump cynically use such language to appeal to his base, or does he genuinely believe what he says? He frequently refers to Senator Warren as Pocahontas, because she once claimed to be part Native American, joking about seeing her on the campaign TRAIL (his capitals). A clear reference to the Trail of Tears—a forced march of Native Americans in the nineteenth century. He said Gonzalo Curiel, a judge of Mexican ancestry, should recuse himself from the Trump University lawsuit because of his Latino heritage. He told four progressive members of Congress to "go back" to the developing countries they came from, whose governments are a "total catastrophe." Three of the four congresswomen were born in the US. At a meeting to discuss immigration, Trump referred to Haiti and African countries as "shit holes." He denied using those words, but several senators recall him using that phrase.

Trump craves constant approval. That is why he took losing the popular vote so hard. How could more Americans vote for "Crooked Hillary" than the man himself? In Trump's mind, they didn't. He has claimed on numerous occasions that the Democrats cheated by the votes of illegal immigrants or by using the details of the deceased. Trump has never produced one shred of evidence to support these claims. He must be the first politician in history to complain about an election he'd won. Likewise, Trump could never accept that more people turned up at Obama's inauguration despite clear photographic evidence. Being sworn in as president would have been the crowning glory of anyone's life, but all he could do was moan about his predecessor. Twice daily, they bring a folder of favourable tweets and press cuttings into the Oval Office. It's a rare read as Trump prefers to watch *Fox News* for hours, the *Pravda* of the modern Republican Party.

Trump's touchy ego means only he can shine. This was what did it for Steve Bannon, the brains behind Trump's victory, whose campaign was floundering before Bannon took it over. The satirical sketch on *Saturday Night Live*, where Bannon was portrayed as the Grim Reaper who controls Trump, so rankled the Great One that Bannon's days were numbered. His need for reassurance reached a nadir in June 2017 when each Cabinet member had to think of something wonderful to say about the president; they tried to outdo the other in sycophancy, while he sat and grinned, unabashed, even elated. This was more in keeping with ageing Communist dictatorships than a democracy. Surely anyone who regularly refers to themselves as a genius (and a stable one to boot) is either delusional or deeply insecure.

Trump does display the characteristics of narcissistic personality disorder (NPD), leading some psychiatrists to question his mental health. Narcissists have delusions about their capabilities and constantly brag about their achievements, even if they are imaginary. They struggle to empathise with others, and need to be constantly in the spotlight. This is to cover a gossamer ego which tolerates no one else shining, apart from them. They love creating disorder and chaos amongst their circle, pitting people against each other. It allows narcissists to stay in control. They will not tolerate criticism and never forget a slight. Now if Trump doesn't have NPD, he does a pretty good impersonation.

But woe betides anyone who fails to praise His Holiness because…

If you're not my friend, then you're my enemy. "With malice toward none" might be all right for Abe Lincoln, but Trump's capacity to bear grudges rivals a Mafia don or Tudor monarch. Trump set the tone in his inauguration speech. Normally a moment of reconciliation, Trump only talked of the "American carnage" that had gone before.

During his term of office, the media, outside his cheerleaders on the right, have come in for particular abuse. Trump dismisses anything disagreeable as "fake news" while journalists who hold him to account are branded "enemies of the American People!" Media outlets he doesn't like are barred from press conferences. Does Trump green light his supporters to use violence? When Rep. Greg Gianforte was found guilty of assaulting a journalist in 2017, Trump didn't see a problem. "Any guy who can do a body slam, he is my type!" The Donald has other ways of intimidating journalists: Dan Heyman was arrested for daring to hold out his phone to Health Secretary Tom Price. The administration also threatened the broadcasting licences of media channels like NBC, who Trump saw as overly critical. The White House even pressured Twitter to reveal private details of an anti-Trump user. Twitter refused. Trump was understandably annoyed—I mean, imagine using Twitter to abuse people!

Trump never forgives a political enemy. John McCain was a particular hate figure for criticising Trump's inflammatory language and policies and blocking the repeal of the Affordable Care Act. Trump was scathing about McCain's bravery when captured during the Vietnam War, he preferred people who "weren't captured." Trump was never captured as he got out of fighting with a medical note for bone spurs, despite being a fine college athlete. Even after McCain died of brain cancer, Trump was not below kicking a dead man. "He was horrible." He said a few months after McCain's funeral.

Trump has lowered America's standing in the world immeasurably. The US has always been respected, though sometimes grudgingly; it was certainly taken seriously and often imitated. But Trump has changed perceptions. In a brilliant article, Irish writer, Fintan O' Toole noted:

> "There is one emotion that has never been directed towards the US until now: pity. However bad things are for most other rich democracies, it is hard not to feel sorry for Americans. Most of them did not vote for Donald Trump in 2016. Yet they are locked down with a malignant narcissist who, instead of protecting his people from Covid-19, has amplified its lethality. The country Trump promised to make great again has never in its history seemed so pitiful."

Second Choice:
History's Worst Vice Presidents

The vice president is rather like the reserve goalkeeper in a soccer team. Someone who sits around with little to do except hope the first choice gets injured. However, jobs have to be found to justify the salary so the Veep attends the funerals of foreign nonentities, or chairs Senate debates. Not surprisingly, the position has rarely attracted America's brightest.

1. Aaron Burr (Democratic-Republican Vice President to Thomas Jefferson 1801–1805)

"A crooked gun, or other perverted instrument, whose aim of shot you could never be sure of."
~ **Thomas Jefferson on Aaron Burr**

Jefferson was speaking metaphorically but it became ironic when Aaron Burr later shot Andrew Hamilton in a duel. Burr deserves the number one spot for being the only vice president to commit murder while in office. He was indicted for the offense in two states, but this

didn't seem to bother anyone as he continued to fulfil his vice-presidential duties.

Burr had higher ambitions. Realizing he had made too many enemies to become president, he still hoped for real political power. So, he hatched a plot to detach and rule the western territory of the USA. Jefferson got wind of this and charged him with treason. But Burr was sensationally acquitted when Jefferson refused to take the witness stand against him. Burr continued his traitorous activities after his term and tried to interest Napoleon in an attack on Boston. Burr then retired to pursue his favourite hobby, womanizing. He had at least two illegitimate children and was a connoisseur of prostitutes. He remarried at seventy-seven to a rich widow forty years his junior, but this ended in divorce on the ground of his continued adultery. On his deathbed, a pastor asked Burr if he believed he was going to Heaven. Burr's reply was, "On that subject I am coy."

2. Henry Wallace (Democrat Vice President to Franklin Roosevelt 1941–1945)

"When I die, I would like to have on my headstone that I was the man who kept Henry Wallace from becoming president..."
~ **Robert Hannegan, Chairman of the Democratic National Committee**

Possibly the strangest vice president, Wallace was greatly admired by his boss, Franklin Roosevelt. Everyone else thought he was completely out to lunch. He was a hippy before the term was invented and liked to indulge in strange cults, earning him the nickname the "Merchant of Globaloney." When Secretary of Agriculture, Wallace financed a mission to find out whether Christ had visited China. What this had to do with American agriculture was anyone's guess, but the Chinese were not amused and arrested Wallace's representative for spying.

He later developed an admiration for Stalin and believed the communist economic model was one America should follow. Roosevelt was finally persuaded to drop him for the 1944 election. It was just as well; Roosevelt died a few months later so Wallace would have succeeded him as president. This Soviet-worshiper wasn't perhaps ideal to face Russia during the Cold War.

3. Spiro Agnew (Republican Vice President to Richard Nixon 1969–1973)

"Spiro Agnew was this country's greatest disaster next to Vietnam."
~ Al Gore

Nixon's creepy Veep got what many thought his boss deserved. He was found guilty of a felony and imprisoned. His impact on the Nixon administration was thankfully minimal. Agnew was usually ignored and White House aides referred to him as "The Clown." His major contribution was to persuade Nixon to bomb Cambodia, a neutral country, in order to win the Vietnam War. In fact, it was this action that convinced many Americans that the US should get out of Indochina ASAP. He later resigned on charges of corruption, dating from his time as Governor of Maryland. Agnew spent his last years as an "international businessman." One of his more profitable deals was selling army uniforms to Saddam Hussein.

4. Charles Curtis (Republican Vice-President to Herbert Hoover 1929–1933)

"(Curtis is) the apotheosis of mediocrity... as devoted to his party as he is dull and dumb."
~ **Oswald Garrison Villard**

A man with some decidedly unpleasant political views, Curtis wouldn't shake hands with African-Americans. He thought the Great Depression was mostly due to the stupidity of ordinary people, and the way for the unemployed to find a job was to get off their butts. At the time, eleven million Americans were out of work.

This didn't go down well with the average voter, struggling through the biggest economic crisis in America's history. In the 1932 election, they decided overwhelmingly to add Curtis to the ranks of the unemployed.

5. Schuyler Colfax (Republican Vice President to Ulysses Grant 1869–1873)

"A little intriguer, aspiring beyond his capacity."
~ **Abraham Lincoln**

Colfax never thought the vice presidency was good enough for his talents and hoped to succeed Grant for the top job when the General grew tired of politics. Unfortunately, Grant grew tired of him first and refused to nominate Colfax for a second term.

Schuyler "The Smiler" had a reputation for shiftiness, and near the end of his vice presidency was caught up in the biggest political scandal of the age. The Credit Mobilier Corporation had overcharged the US Government for building a railroad to the tune of ninety million dollars—a colossal sum in those days. The company then bribed various politicians to keep quiet. One of them was Colfax, who claimed the money had come from a political supporter. This benefactor had subsequently died and Colfax had conveniently forgotten his name. Incredibly, this defence was allowed to stand so Colfax escaped jail.

"Smiler" spent his last years on the lecture circuit giving talks on morality.

6. Dan Quayle (Republican Vice-President to George Bush 1989–1993)

"A callow moron…"
~ **The Philadelphia Daily News**

"The Secret Service is under orders that if Bush is shot, to shoot Quayle."
~ **Anonymous**

Dan Quayle's was, to borrow a phrase from his own Midwest, "too stupid to pour piss out of a boot, even if the instructions were on the heel." There had been plenty of intellectually-challenged politicians in the past, but an unobtrusive media often kept them well hidden. In the modern world, J. Danford Quayle's limitations were cruelly exposed. His main qualifications for Bush's running mate were being reasonably handsome, in a Robert Redford-like way, rich enough to finance much of his campaign, and he was guaranteed to make Bush look like Lincoln.

Pretty soon Quayle's inability to speak or write English made him a national joke. He was unable to spell "potato" during a school visit. On a trip to Latin America, Quayle was supposed to have wished he could speak Latin so he could understand people better. It wasn't true but the fact that this is still widely believed is testimony to his intellectual standing. Here are a few genuine ones: "This election is about who is going to be the next president of the United States." On the San Francisco earthquake of 1990 he declared, "The loss of life will be irreplaceable." Finally, when visiting a South Sea island he said to the natives, "You all look like happy campers to me."

When George Bush was taken ill in Japan, a T-shirt was produced with the image of Edvard Munch's *The Scream*. The writing underneath simply said, "Dan Quayle President." In the 2000 election, Quayle did briefly run for the top job. Sadly, for fans of unintentional comedy, the bid never got off the ground.

7. Hannibal Hamlin (Republican Vice President to Abraham Lincoln 1861–1865)

"I am not consulted at all... (I am) the most unimportant man in Washington, ignored by the President, the Cabinet, and Congress."
~ **Hannibal Hamlin**

Hamlin switched from the Democrats to the Republicans, just as the latter were starting their political ascendancy. His speciality was distributing jobs for votes, and this earned him a place on the Republican ticket of 1860. Hamlin proved an inept choice. He alienated everybody in Washington, especially after he banned alcohol from the Senate—never an institution known for its sobriety. Lincoln chose another vice president for his second term.

Hamlin was given so little to do during his vice presidency that he went back to his farm in Maine. He also volunteered for the local Coast Guard where he rose to the giddy rank of private. He was given catering duties, so Company A of the Maine Coast Guard were astonished to be served ham and eggs by the US vice president. Perhaps he had found his true level of competence.

An interesting footnote: if Lincoln had been shot before his re-election, Hamlin would have become president, earning him overnight promotion from private to five-star general.

8. John Cabal Breckinridge (Democratic Vice President to James Buchanan 1857–1861)

"John Breckinridge, my Joe John
When we first acquaint,
You were an abolitionist,
And now you say you ain't".
~ Popular song

The song sums up Breckinridge's approach to getting elected vice president. Tell the audience whatever they wanted to hear, even if that meant contradicting yourself. It was a smart move in 1856 when America was a bitterly divided nation. The abolitionists were pressing for the ending of slavery throughout the United States. The American South depended on slaves for its huge cotton plantations, and fiercely resisted any policy that might result in their emancipation. Breckinridge's fence jumping was intended to upset as few people as possible. His running mate, James Buchanan, chose to say nothing at all; one opponent joked that he had lockjaw. The strategy worked and Breckinridge became the youngest ever vice president at thirty-eight.

Once in office, Buchanan and Breckinridge continued as the Do-Nothing Party, even though the US was approaching civil war. But when his term ended, Breckinridge declared that slavery was a pretty good thing and the southern states should split from the US. This was from a man who had signed an oath to uphold the Union only four years before. He was later charged with treason and was lucky to escape the gallows after the Union won.

9. George Clinton (Democratic-Republican Vice-President to Thomas Jefferson 1805–1812)

"(Clinton) is old, feeble, and altogether incapable..."
~ A US Senator at the time

During the writing of the Constitution, Clinton was very much against the vice presidency. He thought the office "useless," which is a fair description of Clinton's tenure.

He'd enjoyed a checkered career before being nominated. He'd been an undistinguished general in the American Revolution and a governor in New York's rough and tumble political scene. On at least one occasion Clinton, cheated to remain in power. His main problem as vice president wasn't honesty but senility. Clinton was already seven-four years old when elected, and rapidly losing his grip on events. He frequently miscounted votes in the Senate or forgot whether a law had been passed or not. Incredibly, he was re-nominated for a second term, but old age finally caught up with him in 1812.

One senator summed up the mood of many when he wrote, "A worse choice than Mr Clinton could scarcely (have) been made."

10. Nelson Rockefeller (Republican Vice President to Gerald Ford 1974–1977)

"Take an average American family with an income of one hundred thousand dollars...."
~ Nelson Rockefeller

Rockefeller is on the list as a represent-
tative of those mediocrities that have
inhabited the office—a rather large group
as it happens. Elbridge Gerry, Millard
Fillmore, William Rufus de Vane King (a
silly name seems to be an advantage),
Chester Arthur, Walter Mondale, and a
host of others might also have sufficed.

Rockefeller was heir to one of the largest
fortunes in the world. This gave him
certain advantages over other aspiring
politicians like getting into prestigious
schools despite poor grades. He was made
Assistant Secretary of State for Western Hemisphere Affairs
because the Rockefellers owned large parts of the continent. One
thing his money couldn't buy was the presidency, though he ran
three times. Eventually, he had to settle for the second spot when
Nixon and Agnew resigned.

Rockefeller's main problem was that his wealth—estimated at over
a billion dollars—separated him from the voters. Thinking that the
average person earned a six-figure salary in the 1970s was just one
example. Another was not knowing who James Bond was. He didn't
think this mattered. His attitude resembled the British aristocracy
who believed inherited wealth made you superior to the common
herd. Rockefeller felt ordinary people were unsuited for office as
they were full of "working class resentments." Rockefeller was so
grand he didn't stay in the Vice President's residence because his
own was much better. President Ford felt the working class might
be resentful enough to vote Democrat, so Rockefeller was ditched
from the ticket.

Later, family man Rockefeller died in unusual circumstances. He
had a heart attack while researching a book, though his approach to
writing was somewhat unorthodox. What he was doing with his
twenty-five-year-old blond research assistant, late at night in his
townhouse with no writing materials, remains a mystery.

Divine Wrongs: History's Worst Kings

1. King John (reigned 1189–1216)

"King John was not a good king,
he had his funny ways,
And no one used to talk to him
for days and days and days."
~ **AA Milne**

John wasn't a good king, in both senses, for he was neither kind nor competent. His seventeen-year reign was a mixture of cruelty and failure.

As a youth, he was ignored for much of the time in favour of his three elder brothers, particularly the glamorous Richard the Lionheart. Perhaps this explains the wild bursts of rage and his suspicious, even paranoid, nature. At first there seemed little danger of him inheriting anything. He was derisively nicknamed "Lackland" by his father, Henry II; but with each unfortunate accident John moved nearer to the throne. His eldest brother Henry died of dysentery; Geoffrey was trampled by a horse, which left just Richard in the way. John didn't want to wait for such a technicality as Richard's death; when his brother was captured on his way back from the Crusades, John seized the crown. The resulting lawlessness gave rise to the legend of Robin Hood. Two years later, Richard was released and John begged forgiveness. Richard's opinion of his backstabbing brother can be gathered from his reply, "Think no more of it; John, you are only a child..." John was in his late twenties at the time.

After five more years of waiting, John's luck changed. A fluke arrow hit Richard during a siege and John was king at last. Even his friends (he had some in those days) couldn't quite believe it and giggled during the coronation service in Normandy, especially when John dropped the crown and scepter. It wasn't a good omen.

But John was too sinister to be considered a mere buffoon. When he was campaigning in France, he captured his nephew and rival Arthur of Brittany. Instead of ransoming him (normal for a medieval prince), he had the twelve-year-old murdered in a drunken rage. Even by the low standards of the day, this was too much, and many nobles deserted him for the King of France. In the ensuing war, John was forced out of most of his father's vast continental empire. The ancient link between France and England was gone, and John's reputation never recovered. With his new nickname, "Softsword," he spent much of his time trying to regain his lost territory, but lacked the willpower.

Taxes rose to pay for his campaigns. John was always good at squeezing money out of people. One scheme was forcing noble widows to remarry, then charging them such a fee that they might be financially ruined, leaving John to seize their estates. England's Jewish community particularly suffered. In 1210, they were imprisoned and fined sixty thousand marks. By way of thanks, some had an eye gouged out or gold teeth extracted from their mouths— John anticipated Nazi Germany by over seven hundred years.

Ruthlessness wasn't the real reason for John's unpopularity. It was often part of medieval kingship, though John's cruelty was so random even loyal supporters never felt safe. John's main problem was that he was a failure; whether in diplomacy or domestic rule he always managed to disappoint. Following Henry II brought land and spoils; following John usually brought defeat. His forays in Ireland, Scotland, and Wales (where he cold-bloodedly slew twenty-eight sons of the Welsh nobility) could not make up for the losses in

France. His quarrel with Pope Innocent III over church appointments led to the entire country being denied church services. John was forced to grovel and offer the Pope his kingdom as homage.

By 1214, following another defeat by the French, his barons rose in rebellion and made John sign the Magna Carta. This famous document placed explicit limits on what a king could do. It was the first tentative steps towards constitutional monarchy, so perhaps England should be grateful for John's ineptness. A better king might not have been forced to concede so much.

John died a year later, carried off by dysentery and fever, after gorging himself on peaches. He had been campaigning to crush the baronial rebels. Such was the discontent that some nobles had invited the King of France's son as an alternative candidate. The Barnwell Chronicle wrote, "He had been abandoned before the end by his own people, and in his own end he was little mourned."

2. Nicholas II, Tsar of Russia (r. 1894–1917)

"(Nicholas) would have been an ideal country gentleman, devoting his life to wife and children, his farms and his sport."
~ A friend of the Tsar

"Nicholas II was not fit to run a village post office."
~ Leon Trotsky, an enemy of the Tsar

The Russian Communist leadership used to joke that they should award Nicholas a posthumous Order of the Red Banner (the highest decoration for services to the Revolution) for all he did to help them win power. This dimwit was completely unsuited to guide Russia into the modern world, as it was the modern world he really hated.

If Cher had been alive during Nicholas' reign, her song "Turn Back Time" would have been on his playlist. He wanted his court to imitate his favourite Tsar, Alexis Mikhailovich, who lived in the seventeenth century. He contemplated dressing servants in old-style Kaftans and was only put off by the expense. It's like a modern president suggesting his staffers dress in tricorn hats and knee breeches.

Russia was a growing industrial power, with an increasingly literate urban population. A clash of values was inevitable. In the age of the automobile and the telephone, the Tsar still believed he was divinely appointed to rule over his people as if they were children. The Russian Revolution was one of the most tragic and violent events in world history. It didn't have to be that way, and much of this was due to Nicholas.

3. Gian Gastone de' Medici, Grand Duke of Tuscany (r. 1723 –1737)

The last Medici to rule Florence, Gian Gastone, was a drunk who spent most of the last seven years of his reign in bed. Visiting him required a strong stomach: his boudoir was filled with excrement, puke, and the smell of the dogs. On the rare occasions he ventured out, Gian Gastone made a spectacle of himself by vomiting or uttering obscenities. The Keith Moon of European royalty.

4. Cosimo III, Duke of Tuscany (r. 1670–1723)

The Duchy of Tuscany was in serious decline by the 1670s. Once the financial and artistic capital of Europe, it was now wracked by poverty. What the people needed was an energetic ruler to restore this once proud dukedom. They got Cosimo III instead.

When modern secular states were becoming the norm in Europe, Cosimo wanted to recreate the medieval world of religious fanaticism and brutal punishments. Jews could not walk into the same houses as Christians. Gays were beheaded. Men could not call up to women on balconies (no Romeo and Juliet here). His Medici ancestors had once been patrons to artists like Michelangelo and Leonardo da Vinci. Cosimo III spent his money on holy relics, huge meals, and little clockwork calendars of the saints.

By the time of his death, the population had declined by forty percent.

5. Fyodor I, Tsar of Russia (r. 1584–1598)

Sometimes nature can play cruel tricks. Ivan the Terrible was a vicious but effective ruler. He was tall, physically imposing and smart. His son was, putting it kindly, not so blessed.

In fact, Fyodor I was a moron. His habit of grinning all the time led some to believe he was a fully-fledged simpleton, but others saw his demeanour as holy. There is a long tradition of "saintly fools" in Russia, and Fyodor fitted the bill nicely. Not only by his gurning, but he also loved ringing church bells with anal regularity. Meanwhile, the Russian Court was falling apart. Intrigue and ruthless infighting prefigured a serious conflict, but Fyodor preferred to bell-ring his life away. After his death, Russia was subjected to a fifteen-year civil war called "The Time of Troubles" where a third of the population died.

Fyodor might have been a fool, but he was hardly saintly.

6. Zog I, King of Albania (r. 1928–1939)

"What's going on in Albania...
are you performing a comic opera?"
~ **Kemal Ataturk**

King Zog's reign was as eccentric as his name. He could never decide whether to be Albania's Mussolini or a member of the European royalty. Mostly he resembled Charlie Chaplin in *The Great Dictator*.

Albania had only been independent twelve years before he came to power, but such trivialities never bothered Zog. He claimed his crown was descended from Achilles, Pyrrhus, and Alexander the Great. King Zog started a cult of personality with the fascist trappings of the time. Albanians had to learn a Zogist salute (flat hand over the heart with a downward facing palm, if you want to try it at home); the letter Z was burned into hillsides; and they fined shopkeepers for not putting up his picture.

Although Albania was the poorest country in Europe, Zog still felt he should have a lifestyle appropriate for a monarch. As the *New Yorker* wrote, he turned up for his lavish coronation dressed in "rose-coloured breeches, gold spurs, and a gold crown weighing seven and five-eighths pounds." He also wanted a gaudy summerhouse by the beach. One visitor likened it to a "casino in one of the minor Belgium sea-coast resorts." Taste was something Zog never acquired. He would walk around in a white and gold uniform with a plumed hat until foreign ridicule persuaded him to wear suits.

Zog rarely went abroad because of fears for his safety. These fears proved well founded when someone tried to shoot him on a foreign trip. Instead of running away, Zog took out a revolver and fired back. It's hard to imagine many European monarchs (Queen Victoria, for instance) doing the same. Zog mostly stayed in his palace playing cards, talking (he was a major league tediosity), and smoking up to seven packs of cigarettes a day. When it came to finding a bride, no European royal family was interested. Zog had to be content with a down-on-her-luck Hungarian countess, who was scratching out a living selling postcards.

A year later, Italy invaded Albania to emulate Hitler's military success. Poor Zog never stood a chance. The Albanian air force consisted of two planes, though Zog's appointment of his sisters as army commanders can't have helped.

Zog fled to the US with a sufficient percentage of Albania's wealth to acquire a mansion on Long Island, straight out of *The Great Gatsby*. Bought they said with a "bucket of diamonds and rubies."

7. Richard II, King of England (r. 1377–1399)

Richard II's reign was a case of too much, too young. The story of a spoiled adolescent who grew to become an insufferable adult. King at nine years of age, his finest hour came when he was just fourteen, during the Peasants' Revolt. Ten thousand descended on London demanding an end to the new Poll Tax, which had hit the medieval Joe Sixpacks hard. Much of the nobility fled, but Richard met the rebels face-to-face and agreed to their demands. When the rebels had dispersed, most of the concessions were withdrawn and hundreds were executed.

Richard's ego now reached messianic proportions. He had always believed a king inherited his power from God and was answerable to no one on earth. The Peasants' Revolt had only strengthened this belief. Hadn't the nobles behaved like frightened schoolboys, while he had shown courage beyond his years? This was a huge mistake. More astute monarchs realized they were only as powerful as the lords allowed. Brutalizing peasants was one thing, but annoying the aristocracy was quite another. Yet even the highest lords weren't allowed to look him in the eye, while he was the first English monarch to insist on being called "Majesty." Richard appointed his own supporters to offices the nobles believed were rightly theirs. All this from someone barely out of adolescence.

As he grew older, he got worse. Magnates who had attempted to restrain him were murdered. By the time he was thirty Richard seemed to have established absolute power, but this was an illusion. The nobles were temporarily cowed but not beaten, and they were just waiting for revenge. Their chance came when Richard foolishly banished the most powerful lord in the land, his cousin Henry Bolingbroke, the Duke of Lancaster. This did not go down well, for if he could do this to Bolingbroke who else was safe? When the Duke returned with an army in 1399, support for the king melted away. Richard was forced to abdicate, imprisoned, and then starved to death. A cruel end, but as one chronicler noted at the time, "All the good hearts of the realm clean turned away from him." Shortly afterwards, Bolingbroke was proclaimed Henry IV.

8. Liu He, Emperor of China (r. 74 BCE)

He was left the throne of Han China when his uncle, Emperor Zhao, died. Zhao has fallen out with his son, but the nineteen-year-old Liu He was still an unexpected choice (a case of Liu He, Who He?).

He lost no time in doing what any teenage lottery winner would do. He blew it. During a period of mourning for the old emperor, he started having some serious fun. This was completely against ancient Chinese traditions but... hey, he's the emperor now. Wine, women, and song were the order of the day as friends were promoted and the treasury emptied.

"Tonight we're going to party like it's 74 BCE."

When his aunt, the Dowager Empress, heard she immediately went to the palace. In that tone adults use with teenagers caught sleeping on a bed of beer cans, she fired Liu He. His reign lasted twenty-seven days.

It must have been a great party though.

9. Muhammad II, Shah of Khwarezm (r. 1200–1220)

Genghis Khan. The psychopath's psychopath. A ruler so violent he'd wipe out an entire city if his yak's milk was a bit on the sour side. Not someone you'd want to upset.

So when Genghis offered a decent trade deal to Muhammad II, the Shah of the Khwarazmian Empire (roughly the territory of Greater Iran), you'd have thought he'd grab it with both hands. Not the Shah; after all he was the ruler of Khwarezm, the mighty empire that will last for all eternity. Who was this Mongolian tent dweller, anyway? When Genghis sent some emissaries for trade talks, Muhammad II had them arrested. Remarkably, the Mongol Mr. Big didn't react in his usual way and sent another envoy to say the deal was still on. The Shah executed them, giving a couple of heads back to Genghis as presents.

Genghis Khan's revenge was total. He sent his greatest general, Subutai, and a hundred thousand soldiers to obliterate Khwarezm. They razed every town; the entire population was slaughtered. Salt was mixed into the ground so nothing would grow. The whole civilization was effaced from the world.

He should have signed that trade deal.

10. Philip II, King of Spain (r. 1556–1598)

Philip II inherited the mightiest empire of the sixteenth century. His lands stretched from Tunis to Texas. They included the Netherlands, the commercial centre of Europe, and Spain. His Latin America colonies made Philip as rich as Croesus. But his intense religious faith led to the empire's steep decline.

The gold from the Americas was worth eleven trillion dollars in today's money. But this was frittered away in foreign wars—mostly against those who dared have a different religion than Philip—while he neglected the Spanish economy. High taxes and a tangled bureaucracy didn't help, nor did persecuting Moriscos, the Muslim converts who formed a large part of the business community. Inflation and emigration were rife. He was a religious bigot when fellow rulers—Henry IV of France, Elizabeth I of England, and the Dutch William the Silent—were moving towards toleration. Spain's cultural Golden Age had already begun, but he did his best to shut it down. Spaniards were prevented from studying abroad, cutting off Spain from the currents of European thought. The Spanish Inquisition, the notorious church police, instilled a stultifying conformity. A dislike of modernity pervaded a society where priests and soldiers were honourable callings; they associated businessmen and scientists with foreigners, Protestants, and Jews. The church employed a quarter of the country.

Nothing sums up Philip better than the palace he built. Part monastery, with a basilica at its centre, the Escorial was full of monks and mystics; its floor plan was based on St. Lawrence's grill

PHILIPPVS IIII. DVX BRAB. HISP. II. REX.

(the patron saint of barbecues had been burned to death on a hot grill in the third century). Philip put eight dead relatives in the crypt and, for a pick-me-up, would visit them to remember his own mortality. His collection of holy relics contained hundreds of saints' body parts. Philip II loved his collection like a geek loves his model train set. When he was dying, "He asked, during his final days, to have relics corresponding to his aching limbs directly applied to his open wounds. He claimed that the presence and the contact with a part of Saint Sebastian's knee, one of Saint Alban's ribs, or the arm of Saint Vincent Ferrer, soothed his pains and helped him prepare for the sufferings to come." Philip carried on the Habsburg habit of marrying relatives; three of his four wives were cousins or nieces, which might explain some of his descendants' unusual behaviour.

By the end of his reign, Holland, the most productive part of the empire, had been lost. The English had defeated Philip's "Invincible" Armada, but Spain had lots of new shiny churches. Once the gold and silver starting running out, Spain went into a terminal tailspin.

Cervantes' classic novel *Don Quixote* was written shortly after Philip II died. It is a wonderful symbol of his reign. Don Quixote was a minor noble who still believed it was the Middle Ages. The inability to come to terms with the modern world—that was the legacy of Philip II.

The Greasy Pole:
History's Worst Prime Ministers

"I have climbed to the top of the greasy pole."
~ **Benjamin Disraeli on becoming prime minister**

The prime ministership is the oldest elected office in the world. There have been over fifty of them, so it's not surprising that the quality has ranged from the very good (Churchill, Gladstone, and Attlee) to the okay (Palmerston, Baldwin, and Lord Liverpool) to the downright terrible (see below).

Some avoided the list for doing at least one good thing, like Gordon Brown (his rapid response to the banking crisis of 2018), Arthur Balfour (the 1901 Education Act), or William Grenville (abolishing the slave trade). The following group cannot claim even that.

1. Neville Chamberlain, Conservative (1937–1940)

"[Chamberlain] might make an adequate Lord Mayor of Birmingham in a lean year."
~ **David Lloyd George**

"In the depths of that dusty soul is nothing but abject surrender."
~ **Winston Churchill**

Chamberlain wasn't quite as bad as his reputation stands, but as his reputation is so low, he still comfortably makes the top. His premiership was dominated by one thing, and a very big thing it was too–what should Britain do about Nazi aggression?

And Chamberlain royally screwed up.

If he was in a Shakespearean tragedy, Chamberlain's character flaw would be vanity. Beneath a diffident exterior was a supremely vain man; his letters to his sister, for example, reveal a monstrous ego. He referred to his special magic as, the "Chamberlain touch." He once wrote, "I know I can save this country and I don't believe anyone else can." All this, despite having no foreign policy experience. Bob Boothby MP wrote that "To Baldwin [his predecessor] Europe was a bore, and Chamberlain only a bigger Birmingham." Birmingham was the city where he cut his political teeth.

Chamberlain was meek towards Hitler, but ruthless with anyone who disagreed with him. For how could any reasonable person disagree with the only man who could save Britain? He tended to believe gainsayers were not only wrong, but morally suspect, and were removed from their positions—men like Rex Leeper, a fervent anti-appeaser who was head of the Foreign Office's Press Office. Leeper's crime? He didn't ensure enough sympathetic coverage of the Nazis in the British press. Chamberlain used a former MI5 officer, Sir Joseph Ball, who founded the Conservative Research Department; despite its mild sounding name, this organisation could have taught Nixon's C.R.E.E.P. a thing or two. Ball established a back-channel with the Italian Fascist dictatorship to undermine Foreign Minister Anthony Eden's attempts to oppose Mussolini's increasing aggression; this forced Eden's resignation who was replaced by the pliant Lord Halifax. Ball leaned on Conservative newspapers to provide pro-appeasement and even pro-German views. He secretly acquired the magazine *Truth* to traduce the reputation of those who opposed appeasement, especially Churchill. All this with the prime minister's approval. Chamberlain even had Ball tap anti-appeasing Tories' phones. He boasted to his sister that overheard calls "demonstrated how completely Winston can deceive himself."

It was Chamberlain who was deceiving himself. His ruthlessness, which tested the boundaries of legality, might have been excusable in a crisis if Chamberlain had been right. But even after it was clear Hitler was planning imperial conquest, even after the unjustifiable invasion of Czechoslovakia, even when British public opinion then turned against appeasement, Chamberlain wouldn't budge. That would mean he was wrong, and that kind of self-awareness was beyond him.

As Europe headed for war, Chamberlain wrote to his sister that "all the information I get seems to point in the direction of peace." The bullying of recalcitrant MPs by the Whips' Office continued, as did secret missions to Germany behind the foreign secretary's back. Chamberlain even encouraged the openly pro-Nazi Drummond Wolff to smooth things over with Goering. The Nazis regarded Chamberlain as a poltroon they patronised and exploited, while he clung to his belief that somehow the "Chamberlain touch" would avert war. And every week, planes and Panzers rolled off German production lines.

Chamberlain's supporters produced two arguments in his defence. He started Britain's rearmament programme that produced RADAR, the Spitfire that helped to win the war, and he brought us a crucial year at Munich in the autumn of 1938, so we were better prepared when the war came. Neither holds up to examination. The rearmament programme was inadequate, hobbled by budgetary restraint and a lack of will. In March 1938 the British Expeditionary Force had only three divisions and insufficient anti-aircraft guns; by October two Spitfires were ready. However, the overall Allied strength was still greater than Germany's during the Munich crisis. Germany had only six weeks of ammunition. Their Great West Wall defence system against France was a building site defended by eight divisions, whereas the French had twenty-three. Add to that thirty-four well-equipped Czech divisions and their formidable defensive system, plus a potential Soviet alliance, as Stalin had not yet decided who to support. Generals Jodl and Manstein later admitted they thought Germans would have lost in 1938.

A year later, partly thanks to the "Chamberlain touch," Czechoslovakia was occupied, and its huge resources and armament works taken by the Nazis. The Soviet had signed a peace agreement with Hitler, and Germany had comfortably outspent Britain and France in war preparations—for instance, the Luftwaffe had expanded by five times. Chamberlain never intended the Munich Agreement to buy time; rather it was a permanent peace, which explains why he was the least enthusiastic military spender in the Cabinet during 1939.

When war came, he was the wrong man to inspire Britain to fight, and after the debacle in Norway (ironically Churchill's fault) he resigned. He was loyal to Churchill in the last few months of his life when others weren't, but this cannot erase the immense harm he'd done to his country, and the world, during his premiership.

2. Lord North, Whig then Tory (1770–1782)

"We must shew (sic) the Americans that we will no longer fit quite under their insults..."
~ **Lord North**

He lost America.

Think about it. The most valuable piece of real estate Britain ever owned, and he lost it. He can't be solely blamed; there were others, but he was prime minister during the slide to war and throughout its incompetent prosecution: the Boston Tea Party (he was the one who refused to scrap the tea duty), the

Intolerable Acts, Concord, all under North. He refused to listen to Pitt and compromise with the colonists, and then right at the end of his tenure came up with a plan that would have avoided war a few years earlier—but by this time America was intent on independence.

"Oh God! It is all over!" was Lord North's remark on hearing of Britain's defeat at Yorktown. And it was, for British colonial rule and his career.

3. David Cameron, Conservative (2010–2016)

"While parents worried about childcare, getting the kids to school, balancing work and family life, we were banging on about Europe."
~ **David Cameron**

Mary Tudor said that after she died, they would engrave Calais on her heart, so grievously did she mourn the loss of English's last continental territory. No prizes for guessing what we'll write on Cameron's. He wanted to wean the Tories off their obsession with Europe, but he ended up engulfing his party and the nation over the issue.

Cameron looked the part. He exuded the easy charm of the aristocracy but was like a swan who glides effortlessly on the water but is frantically kicking below the surface. Lazy, and with a tendency to panic, Cameron usually backed down. He was more like some upper-class 19th-century dilettante, who plays at politics for a while before making serious money in the city. This lack of backbone encouraged his Eurosceptic wing to push for more and more concessions until they got the big one: a referendum on British membership of the European Union. Why did he hock the future of the nation on something he knew was wrong? Cameron claimed it was because people wanted the vote, but polls at the time don't support this. One showed that only ten per cent of voters said Europe was one of the top three issues compared with 65 per cent citing the economy, 35 per cent health, and 32 per cent pensions. It was more about his own party's preservation of power. He was seriously unnerved by the rise of the populist UKIP, and he thought it would buy off some of his restlessness backbenchers. We now know Cameron thought he would never have to honour this pledge, as he never expected to win a majority in the next parliament; when he did win one in 2015, he had to honour a promise he'd never intended to keep.

Even then, Cameron fought with one hand tied behind his back—he'd tied the knots himself—while his opponents came with knuckledusters. He let Brexit ministers openly campaign for Leave, which surprised them as they had expected to be sacked. He refused to extend the franchise to 16 and 17 years-olds, even though a precedent had been set in the Scotland Referendum. He later admitted the mistake, as they would have overwhelmingly voted Remain. He let Leavers dictate the timetable. The original date of 2017 would have suited him better, allowing him time for his European reforms to take hold. All of this points to a man who put party before country.

This most cowardly of prime ministers was the first casualty of Brexit when he resigned on the morning after the Referendum. On his last day, Cameron quoted Enoch Powell's dictum, "All political lives end in failure." Particularly if you're as spineless as me, he might have added.

4. Anthony Eden, Conservative (1955–1957)

"Eden... destroyed (his reputation as a peacemaker) and led Great Britain to one of the greatest humiliations in her history... He acted impatiently and on impulse. Previously flexible, he now relied on dogma, denouncing Nasser as a second Hitler... The outcome was pathetic rather than tragic."
~ **AJP Taylor**

"I don't believe Anthony can do it."
~ **Churchill's private remarks to his secretary about Eden's potential as the prime minister**

With Eden, the whole was always much less than the sum of the parts. He seemed a perfect choice for premier. A brilliant military career, a Military Cross winner, he was the youngest brigade major in World War 1. Good-looking and cultured (he wrote about and collected art), he was a brilliant linguist (fluent in Persian, French, German, and Arabic) and a Cambridge double first. He was one of the few British politicians to emerge with any credit from the 1930s, opposing appeasement, though not with quite the consistency some of his supporters claim. What went wrong? The Suez Crisis, when Eden's misjudgement and mendacity led Britain to international humiliation.

Colonel Nasser, the new leader of Egypt, nationalised the Suez Canal in 1956. This threatened British oil supplies and her standing in the Middle East, but Eden's response was disproportionate. He hatched a plot with France and Israel to fix Nasser. Israel invaded the Sinai which Britain and France then used as an excuse to occupy the Canal Zone. It was a military success and a diplomatic disaster. The Soviets threatened nuclear war and President Eisenhower told Eden the US would ensure sterling's collapse if Britain didn't withdraw, which it did with its tail between its legs. Sylvia Ellis wrote that Suez "signified the end of Great Britain's role as one of the world's major powers." The US could sink the British economically in a matter of days, while former colonies could openly defy her. The days of sending gunboats to teach Johnny Foreigner a lesson were over. During the Suez Crisis, international attention in the Middle East encouraged the Soviets to invade Hungary and crush the lone democratic experiment behind the Iron Curtain. Britain could hardly criticise Russia for invading another country.

Why did such an experienced politician, whose specialism was foreign affairs, make such a terrible mistake? He was no fanatical imperialist. He was a believer in the United Nations and the international rule of law, and his attorney general had told him the intervention was probably illegal. But Eden had developed a visceral hatred for Nasser, who he saw as another Hitler. "I want him destroyed; can't you understand? I want him murdered," he told a minister. This was uncharacteristic of Eden, leading some historians to speculate that his declining health played a part. He was suffering from a failed operation and dependent on amphetamines to function.

The other bad decision during his brief tenure might have had even worse consequences. He was prime minister during the Messina Conference in 1955, which formed the nucleus of the European Union. They invited Britain to join subsequent discussions, but Eden refused to attend. He had no time for an integrated Europe. "Our thoughts move across the seas to the many communities in which our people play their part in every corner of the world…" he remarked. Would things have been different if Britain had helped shape the course of Europe instead of joining much later? We shall never know.

5. Thomas Pelham-Holles, Duke of Newcastle
(Whig, 1754–1756, 1757–1762)

"The epitome of unredeemed mediocrity and as a veritable buffoon in office."
~ **Harry Dickinson, historian**

"He had no pride, though infinite self-love."
~ **Horace Walpole**

The Duke is a classic example of a loyal lieutenant who spent years pleasing the boss and then is exposed when he finally runs the show. Newcastle earned a reputation as a master of patronage in an age of corruption. Years before the secret ballot, they brought votes for favours, and he was perhaps British politics' greatest briber. If that's a title to be proud of.

Newcastle was a Whig in the partisan, violent early 18th century. He helped organise groups of thugs, called "Newcastle mobs" to beat up Tories (admittedly the Tories were also happy to mete out kickings). Newcastle quickly attached himself to the coming man, Robert Walpole. A smart move, Walpole was the longest-serving prime minister in history and every bit as corrupt as Newcastle. Walpole's motto was, "Every man has his price" and in those days this was probably true. Walpole and Newcastle ensured that the trough was full enough to stay in power for over 20 years.

Nothing was allowed to get in the way of Newcastle's ambition. When his relative and fellow Whig minister, Charles Townshend, fell out with Walpole, Newcastle put career before family and sided with the prime minister. When Walpole's fell, Newcastle nimbly switched to another winning horse—his own brother. Walpole's son never forgave him. When it was Newcastle's turn, he proved a better follower than a leader. He failed to prevent the French and Indian War, despite foreign policy being his area of expertise, which initially went so badly for Britain there were calls for his execution. They shot an admiral instead, after the loss of Minorca, though many felt they'd executed the wrong man. Newcastle was driven from office but returned eight months later. The war went better but largely because once more he had someone to rely on: William Pitt, who really ran operations, persuading a reluctant Newcastle that military victory lay in North America, not Europe. So dominant was Pitt that it is often incorrectly stated that he was the prime minister during the war (he was leader of the House of Commons). Newcastle, though PM, did what he was best at, serving others.

6. F. J. Robinson, 1st Viscount Goderich, (Tory, 1827–1828)

"A damned, snivelling, blubbering blockhead."
~ **George IV**

"Never surely was there a man at the head of affairs so weak, undecided, and utterly helpless."
~ **William Huskisson on Goderich**

Goderich enjoys the dubious distinction of being the shortest-serving prime minister who didn't die in office. Like most PMs of the time, he owed his ascent to family connections. A member of the landed aristocracy, his mother's cousin helped shin him up the greasy pole. He had a competent administration, but when he became prime minister, his tenure was as unhappy as it was brief. Goderich could not form a workable coalition between Whigs and moderate Tories. His main problem was his own weakness: caught between an interfering George IV, who regarded Goderich with undisguised contempt, and discontented Whigs pressing for more power. He failed to stand up to either. His wife's descent into mental illness didn't help, and after four months he threw in the towel. He burst into tears when offering his resignation to the king. A few weeks later he had noticeably perked up; released from an office he never wanted, and for which he was manifestly unsuited.

7. Theresa May (Conservative, 2016-2019)

"She must be the only leader in living memory who has tried to fall on her own sword and managed to miss."
~ Nicola Sturgeon

In this era of 24/7 news and social media, the relentless scrutiny of prime ministers soon exposes their flaws. This was never more so than with Theresa May. She started well enough. On her first day, she made a direct appeal for unity after the bitter Brexit Referendum and promised to confront the "burning injustices" of modern Britain. Alas, it was not to be. The more people saw, the less they liked Theresa. As with Chamberlain, her quiet veneer hid a fiercely partisan, intolerant politician who failed to achieve a national consensus over Brexit. Suspicious and cliquey, she found it difficult enough to work with members of her own party, let alone reach across the political divide. This would prove fatal when May lost her majority in an election she swore she'd never call. After that, she was on borrowed time, but old habits die hard and May could not bring herself to compromise; her Brexit deal was rejected by the greatest parliamentary margin in modern times. She'd been unwilling to cultivate potential allies in other parties, and she'd insisted on sticking to her red lines in negotiations, as if they were Holy Scripture rather than a set of unworkable and contradictory proposals.

Part of the problem was May tried to micromanage the whole government with a few trusted advisors. We were "overwhelmed," said her chief of staff, Nick Timothy. "The role of the prime minister is not to play every instrument in the orchestra but to write the score and conduct the musicians. Too often, May was trying to play the strings, woodwind, brass, and percussion all at the same time." This was made worse by her tendency to dither over decisions. Unsurprising, she achieved little in three unproductive years. Despite her promise to tackle injustices, poverty increased at its highest rate in thirty years, and people who had lived here for decades found themselves denied medical care or deported during the Windrush Scandal.

There was a cowardly side too. May was nicknamed "the Submarine" as home secretary because she'd only surface when it was safe to do so. If you wanted a minister to face tough questioning on TV about a difficult subject, don't call Theresa. When she was prime minister, a London council block, Grenfell Tower, burnt down. She refused to meet the survivors at first because of how angry they were feeling—citing "security" concerns. Seventy-two people had been burnt to death; many were relatives and friends, and now these survivors were being lumped as potential terrorists. It was an act of breath-taking callousness. She admitted later this was her biggest regret. During the election campaign of 2017, she spent much of her time avoiding the public. She even ducked the leaders' debate (after all, the voters might have the temerity to ask difficult questions.) and sent one of her ministers, Amber Rudd, instead. What didn't seem to bother Theresa May was that Rudd had just lost her father forty-eight hours before.

And Theresa's re-election slogan? She promised "strong and stable" leadership.

8. Jim Callaghan (Labour, 1976–1979)

"I think we are all re-evaluated as time goes by and I should not be the slightest bit surprised if there is another evaluation after I die and people come to the conclusion that I was the worst prime minister since Walpole."
~ **Jim Callaghan**

Timing is as important for politicians as comedians. Get it right, and you're a brilliant statesman; get it wrong and, well, ask "Sunny Jim" Callaghan.

In the summer of 1978, he had been prime minister for two years. They'd been difficult times. Britain had borrowed money from the IMF. Strikes and sharp price rises had bedevilled the economy, but things had turned around. Inflation was down, and living standards up. The Labour government had recovered in the polls and were leading the Conservative opposition. What's more, Callaghan was well-liked. Brits took to his easy-going, amiable personality far more than his starchy, rather abrasive opponent, Margaret Thatcher. He was hugely experienced and, by all accounts, an able administrator. The only prime minister to have held all three major cabinet positions—chancellor, foreign secretary, and home secretary. Some polls gave him a 20-point lead on who would make the best prime minister.

The expectations mounted of an early election when Callaghan could cash in on his popularity; the venue was to be the Trade Union Conference in September 1978, but instead of announcing the date, he burst into an old music hall song:

"There was I waiting at the Church, waiting at the Church, waiting at the Church,

When I found he'd left me waiting in the lurch, Lor' how it did upset me.

All at once, he sent me round a note. Here's the very note; this is what he wrote,

'Can't get away to marry you today. My wife won't let me.'"

People were not clear what he meant for a few days. Was he delaying an election? Mocking the opposition for not being ready? Callaghan was, in fact, putting off the vote until Spring, with disastrous consequences. Strikes spiked in the Winter of Discontent. Union leaders were angry at his procrastination and demand for public sector pay restraint. Rubbish piled up on the streets as council workers struck. Even gravediggers in Liverpool and Manchester downed tools. In parts of the country, you couldn't get either your dead granny or your rubbish cleared. It was ironic because Callaghan was always seen as the trade unions' main political backer, who'd defeated earlier reforms to curb their power; some of which would have reduced the strikes that were destroying his administration.

The images on TV were terrible. Callaghan exacerbated things when he went to a conference in the Caribbean and told the press how he'd enjoyed swimming there; while Britain suffered a freezing and strike-prone winter. "Sunny Jim" no longer seemed such an endearing sobriquet. By the end of February, Labour was almost 20 points behind the Tories and went on to defeat in May. It took 18 years for Labour to return to power; the memories of the last few months of Callaghan's prime ministership were partly responsible.

9. Duke of Wellington (Tory, 1828–30, 1834)

"An extraordinary affair. I gave them their orders and they wanted to stay and discuss them."
~ **Duke of Wellington**

Britain has been spared the tradition of military men becoming politicians. After the brief, unhappy rule of the Duke of Wellington, it can count itself lucky.

His generalship, particularly his victory over Napoleon at Waterloo, made him a national hero but he never really got the hang of politics, as the quote above shows. He expected to run his government like his campaigns. When he became prime minister in 1828, the Tories had been in power for years, but they were tired, divided, and much of their talent had died. His high-handedness drove many Tories to join the Whigs and left him with a minority government.

Wellington was also on the wrong side of public opinion on the main issue of the day: reforming the voting system (barely ten per cent of the male population had the vote.) His opposition to it frittered away the popularity he had earned as a general—missiles were thrown at his house. Lacking support in Parliament he resigned in 1830 on the death of George IV, and the energized Whigs won the general election by a landslide. The Tories received less than 30 per cent of the vote and were out of power for a decade. Ever the snob, Wellington was disgusted by the influx of MPs after the new franchise. "I never saw so many shocking bad hats in my life," he remarked.

His support for Catholic Emancipation in 1829 almost saves Wellington from the list, but his opposition to giving Jews more rights puts him on again.

10. Lord Salisbury
(Conservative, 1885–1892, 1895–1902)

"Deeply neurotic, depressive, agitated, introverted, fearful of change and loss of control, and self-effacing but capable of extraordinary competitiveness."
~ **Paul Smith**

He is on the list for what he didn't do. Britain was badly in need of reform as the 19th century drew to a close, but Salisbury made a point of doing as little as possible. It was his raison d'être for staying in power. "Whatever happens will be for the worse, and therefore it is in our interest that as little should happen as possible..." he remarked.

This was a shame because he was a towering figure in both senses of the word, as he stood 6 foot four inches and possessed a brilliant mind. His ancestor was Queen's Elizabeth I's chief minister, William Cecil, and he shared some of his distant relative's political talents. Unlike William, however, he clung to a vision of the past rather than trying to mold the future. Robert Blake, the Conservative historian, wrote that "he was the most formidable intellectual figure that the Conservative party has ever produced" but agreed that he was "essentially negative, indeed reactionary in domestic policy."

And there was much to be done. Poverty was widespread in Britain, despite having the largest empire the world had ever seen and an advanced industrial economy. Infant mortality was higher than in 1800. During the Boer War (1899–1902) potential recruits were rejected on health grounds; in a city like Manchester, up to half the men who volunteered could not pass the low-level medical examination. Salisbury dismissed help to the poor as socialistic, the views of an 18th-century squire, not a prime minister in an age of electricity.

Salisbury had definite opinions about extending the franchise as well—the masses were fine as servants or grouse beaters, but he was implacably against allowing them to vote. Nor was his animus confined to the working class. When an aspiring politician of Indian origin narrowly lost an election, he commented, "I doubt if we have yet got to the point where a British constituency will elect a black man to represent them," which earned a rebuke from Queen Victoria.

Ireland was another bugbear. Overwhelmingly, the country wanted Home Rule, modelled on Canada's relationship with Britain. In opposition, Salisbury used the Conservative dominance of the Lords to stop such a bill from passing; in government, he wanted to kill Home Rule "with kindness" by launching a land reform programme. It was too little, too late, and it failed to buy off most people. The delay meant that when Home Rule passed, sectarian hatreds between Catholics and Protestants had considerably increased and a peaceful transition was impossible. Salisbury contributed to the bloody years to come.

He had a reputation as a great trencherman and died from difficulties breathing because of his massive weight. Clearly, the malnourishment of many fellow citizens didn't affect him. Salisbury estate was worth £33,000,000 in today's money–largely from inheritance, like most of the landed aristocracy.

In one sense he could be counted a success; he achieved his aim of holding back reforms for years. But he was like the legend of King Canute trying to stop the tide. He left the premiership to his nephew, Arthur Balfour (the phrase *Bob's Your Uncle* stems from this, even in the Edwardian age such nepotism was too much), and the 1906 election saw the largest ever swing to the Liberal Party. The reforms that Salisbury hated could now begin.

Tiny Platoons:
History's Dumbest Political Parties

There's been enough of them.

This list excludes history's nastiest political parties. Otherwise, the Nazis and the Bolsheviks would be at the top. Nor does it include joke parties formed for fun or to satirize the political system, like the Friends of Beer Party (Czech Republic) or the Union of Conscientiously Work-Shy Elements (Denmark). Rather, it comprises useless political movements that took themselves seriously but never achieved power; the list is distinguished by political failure and idiocy.

1. The Prohibition Party, USA

"A great social and economic experiment."
~ Herbert Hoover

Perhaps the Prohibition Party wasn't a failure. After all, its main policy was put into practice: the production and sale of alcohol were banned, first at the state level and then nationally, when the 18th Amendment was ratified in 1919. That's when their problems started. Prohibition proved such a ridiculous idea. It has become a byword for a misguided law and is still frequently cited as an argument not to ban anything. The 18th also has the distinction of being the only constitutional amendment to be repealed. True, alcohol consumption and related illnesses declined; it is a popular myth that they didn't, but it proved a major boost for organised crime and corrupted many municipal police forces. It led to a fall in tax revenues when they were badly needed during the Great Depression and encouraged ordinary people to break the law.

117

Prohibition's promise of the moral regeneration of America was hard to find in the world of speakeasies and Al Capone.

Undeterred by its failure, the Prohibition Party continues to fight the good fight under the slogan, "Character, Hope, Tradition." In the 2016 presidential election, it polled 5,617 votes.

2. Know-Nothing or American Party, USA

"All Catholics and all persons who favour the Catholic Church are...vile imposters, liars, villains, and cowardly cutthroats."
~ **Know-Nothing Poster in Boston**

It's a sad but familiar picture. A rise in immigration is met by hostility from the native population. Never mind that these immigrants were vital to America's expanding economy, or that the natives were from families that had once been immigrants themselves. The American Party, as they were officially known, came out of secret societies like the Order of the Star-Spangled Banner, formed as a reaction to the influx of Catholic Irish and German immigrants from the 1820s. They thrived on a toxic mix of conspiracy theories and racial stereotyping. These movements often do. Their nickname came from their secretive nature, when asked what they stood for they often replied, "I know nothing."

The party grew quickly, helped by the decline of the Whigs and the splits in the Democrats. At one point they had fifty-two Congressmen in the House of Representatives and controlled the Massachusetts state legislature. However, their rise was accompanied by violence against Catholics, the worst being in Louisville, Kentucky, where twenty-two were killed. In Philadelphia they burned down a Catholic Church.

The Know-Nothing's decline was as rapid as its ascent. Poor leadership didn't help, but sectional differences broke them. Proslavery southerners joined the Democrats while northerners helped form the new Republican Party.

3. Cornish Nationalist Party, United Kingdom

Not to be confused with the bigger Party for Cornwall. They used to be a single group but split in a Pythonesque "Popular Front of Judea" moment in the 1970s. The CNP supports the development of the Cornish language despite no one speaking it, and each year commemorates former Cornish rebel, Thomas Flamank. He was executed a mere 523 years ago by Henry VII, an event that still ignites the whole of Cornwall with indignation. Amazingly, their electoral results have been underwhelming. The CNP never polled over 1.0 per cent in the first three times they stood. They then stopped fighting elections for twenty years. But things are looking up. They recently won a local council seat. The Independent Republic of Cornwall is only a matter of time, with Flamank Day as the national holiday.

4. Anti-Masonic Party, USA

Social media has ensured a golden age for conspiracy theories, but they're nothing new. One of the most prominent parties of the antebellum Republic was based on one. The Anti-Masonic Party was formed after the disappearance of William Morgan in 1826, a former Mason who had become a prominent critic. They did surprisingly well for a while, helped by that unstable political decade after the end of the Federalist Party. People were looking for something new to vote for and the Anti-Masonic Party's railed against the elites—who were not just behind Morgan's demise but everything else wrong with the US. This did them no harm at the ballot box, winning representation in Pennsylvania and Rhode Island. They even received 7.8 per cent of the popular vote in the

1832 presidential election. But single-issue parties always have a limited shelf-life in the US; and the new kid on the block, the Whigs, comfortably eclipsed the Anti-Masonic Party. The Whigs took votes and members from them and by 1840 they had pretty well subsumed the Anti-Masons, winning the presidency with a former party member, William Henry Harrison. The Anti-Masons did leave one permanent mark on US politics—nominating conventions.

5. Public Safety Democratic Monarchist, White Resident Party, United Kingdom

The party's title covered some bases. It was the one-man band of British eccentric/lunatic, Colonel Bill Boaks; holder of the record for the joint lowest vote ever received in a by-election (five, Glasgow Hillhead, 1982). This did not faze him. He once said, "I have never bothered about votes. The thing that matters is to give people the chance to vote; it is a matter of complete indifference to me how they vote as long as they have a choice." There was always

something comically inept about Colonel Boaks. He first stood against the then Prime Minister Clement Attlee, only to find he had picked the wrong constituency. Attlee was MP for Walthamstow West, not Walthamstow East. Normally the British like this; in no other country would Eddie "the Eagle" Edwards (perhaps the worst competitive ski-jumper in history) be a national hero. However, the "White Monarchist" tag smacked too much of the rising racist tide in the 1970s and 80s for Brits to take him to heart. He always claimed it was never meant in that way, but a description of what he was. He then offered a pound and said, "Now find 149 more [the price of a candidate's deposit was £150] of those and stand as a "Black Immigrant" candidate for what you believe in. If you don't, who will?" Boaks' views ranged from left to right, but one issue dominated his campaigns: road safety. It became an obsession. He would push a brick-laden pram onto pedestrian crossings to stop vehicles, as he believed cars should not have the right of way. He tried to sue public figures who had been involved in road accidents, including Prince Philip and Attlee's wife, and was arrested several times for deliberately obstructing traffic—once at the England versus Scotland football match when he refused to move his van until all the pedestrians had crossed. Ironically, he died in 1984 after suffering injuries in two road accidents.

The Minister for Transport attended his funeral.

6. Veritas, United Kingdom

Robert Kilroy-Silk was a TV personality with an outsized ego who thought this could translate into political success. I mean, that ludicrous idea could never happen, could it? Kilroy-Silk had been a Labour MP who gave up his seat to host a daytime TV show, *Kilroy,* in 1986. He was a natural and the show ran for 18 years. Missing politics, he successfully stood as a MEP for the UK Independence Party in 2004. Again, this was a smart move. UKIP was rising in the polls and his celebrity status didn't hurt either. But Kilroy Silk now figured what UKIP needed was a leader with a national profile and selflessly pushed himself forward. Other members were nonplussed that a man who had joined less than a year before was now trying to take over the party. His bid was blocked, and he flounced off to form Veritas. This wasn't such a smart move. Critics quickly dubbed the party Vanitas. Kilroy Silk finished a distant fourth in Erewash in the next general election. He then quit and Veritas stumbled on for another ten years before giving up the ghost, never getting over five per cent of the vote. What they stood for was little more than a collection of bar-room prejudices, like several minor British parties. And Kilroy-Silk? They cancelled his last TV show after only four episodes.

7. Vegetarian Party, USA

Formed by naturopathic doctors in 1947, when eating steak was practically a constitutional right, they were regarded as at best, eccentric, and at worst, a communist front. This was the year Senator Joe McCarthy was first elected. The Vegetarian Party did nominate presidential and vice-presidential candidates until 1964 without setting any of these races on fire. The idea of vegetarianism has gained credence in recent years, but their other major plank is perhaps a ways off. They were also against the use of medicine.

8. Party of Right and Legality (PLL), Albania

In Europe's fragmented political landscape minor parties can thrive, especially when politicians are elected by proportional representation. There are dozens of fringe movement that can amass a few seats but have little hope of achieving their program. The PLL is chosen as a representative of this, and because it has a particularly brainless cause: the restoration of the Albanian monarchy under King Zog's son, Leka. After the hapless Zog you'd think they'd be breathing a sigh of relief, but this didn't stop the PLL arguing for Zog 2.0. True to his family's eccentricity, Leka didn't vote for the PLL stating, "I am above party politics, even my own."

9. The Party for God, Peace and Unification, South Korea

Chosen for the rampant egotism of the leader and the gullibility of its followers, the Moonies were a South Korean cult, famous for mass weddings and Messianic worship of its founder, the Reverend Sun Myung Moon. Amassing great wealth and adulation wasn't enough for the former Presbyterian Sunday school teacher. He wanted political influence. In 2003 he formed the Party for God, Peace and Unification, to unite the Korean peninsula and bring peace to the world. Failure to achieve this aim didn't stop the reverend receiving a "Prince of Peace" crown a year later. Who awarded such a prestigious title? Have a guess.

10. Ralph Nader and the Green Party, United States

"His public appearances during the campaign, far from brutally honest, were larded with dissembling, prevarication and demagoguery..."
~ **Jonathan Chait**

Ralph Nader has much to be proud of. His advocacy of environmental causes, consumer protection, and automobile safety has led to significant legislation. However, his presidential bid in 2000 helped put a man in the White House who stood for everything Nader opposed. Nader was warned that in such a tight contest he might take votes away from Al Gore and give George W. Bush victory. And this is exactly what happened. In the crucial state of Florida, Bush won by 537 votes, where Nader received over 90,000. Independent research suggests that most of those votes would have gone to Gore. Nader was, at the time, even suggesting he would have voted for Bush rather than Gore as federal agencies would fare better under Dubya. Odd considering that Gore's prominent advocacy of environmental issues was similar to Nader and Bush was a climate-change denier. The journalist Marianne Means later wrote, "[Nader's] candidacy was based on the self-serving argument that it would make no difference whether Gore or George W. Bush were elected. This was insane. Nobody, for instance, can imagine Gore picking as the nation's chief law enforcement officer a man of [John] Ashcroft's anti-civil rights, antitrust, anti-abortion and anti-gay record. Or picking Bush's first choice to head the Labor Department, Linda Chavez, who opposes the minimum wage and affirmative action."

Idiots-in-Chief:
History's Worst Generals

"Brains! I don't believe in brains."
~ The Duke of Cambridge Commander-in-Chief of the British
Army (1856–1895)

"There are no bad soldiers, only bad officers."
~ Napoleon Bonaparte

1. Adolf Hitler, World War II (1939–1945)

Surely history's worst commander. At the start of World War II, Hitler took control of the German armed forces. In what was called the "Fuhrer Principle," a failed artist and former World War I messenger boy ran one of the most complex war machines in history. Don't believe the evil genius myth that Hitler was brutal but brilliant. What strikes you is the sheer knuckle-headed stupidity of most of his decisions. Here are just a few Fuhrer Failures:

The "First Soldier of the Reich" replaced the General Staff with talentless yes men and Nazi ideologues.

Hitler didn't invest in the Germany nuclear program, dismissing physics as a "Jewish science."

A belief in instinct rather than careful planning resulted in ridiculous decisions and avoidable failures.

Switching to the bombing of civilian targets during the Battle of Britain gave the RAF a respite and helped them ultimately win the air battle.

He launched suicidal attacks against numerically superior opponents, as in the tank Battle of Kursk or in the Ardennes against the US.

He declared war on the US after Pearl Harbor to raise German morale (good call).

Invading Russia (never invade Russia, ask Napoleon) made worse by his refusal to retreat at Stalingrad, ensured the destruction of his crack Sixth Army.

Turning the ME262, perhaps the best fighter plane of the war, into a bomber, was like training a greyhound for bear baiting.

His racial theories stopped Germany working with Slavs willing to fight against the Soviet Union.

He failed to employ enough women in the war industries because he didn't believe women should work (no Reni the Riveter in the Third Reich).

Micromanaging the war from an isolated bunker prevented individual initiatives; even an armoured car sometimes had to wait for permission to retreat.

His tenuous grip on reality had departed by the end as he ordered phantom regiments, already destroyed, into the fray.

None of his foam-flecked rages could disguise the fact the Hitler was an amateur in a highly skilled professional. Save the evil genius for Bond movies.

2. General Ambrose Burnside, American Civil War (1861–1865)

"I do not want command. I am not competent to command such a large army!"
~ General Burnside

Well, at least he was honest, but he still accepted command of the Unionist forces during the Civil War. At the Battle of Fredericksburg, he attacked the Confederates by crossing the Rappahannock River in the middle of winter, even though the current was obviously strong.  His men then had to charge up a ridge to well-fortified grey-back positions. He then ordered them to charge fourteen times until a subordinate officer called off the attack—unable to stomach any more casualties. Burnside accused his men of cowardice and then broke down and cried. In a ridiculous gesture for a commander, he offered personally to lead his old unit.

At Antietam he ordered his men to cross a narrow bridge instead of fording shallow water, therefore providing easy targets for the enemy. Lincoln ruefully wrote, "Only Burnside could have managed such a coup, wringing one last spectacular defeat from the jaws of victory."

3. General Antonio Santa Anna, Texas Revolution (1835–1836) and the Mexican-American War (1846–1848)

He styled himself the "Napoleon of the West"' but his military skills were closer to Napoleon Dynamite than the Little Corporal. Vain and cruel, he's best remembered for his assault on the Alamo during the Texas Revolution. Yet the fort was of little strategic value and delayed the Mexican advance. His killing of Texans in cold blood caused such outrage that many flocked to their cause.

Worse was to come. At the Battle of San Jacinto much of his army was caught napping, literally. Instead of posting guards, he let Texan soldiers surprise his men during their afternoon siesta. The eighteen-minute battle saw Santa Anna desert his men disguised as a private. Very Napoleonic.

1846 and Round Two—the Mexican-American War. Santa Anna was once more in charge, much to the relief of the US. He now sported a cork leg after fighting in the wonderfully named Pastry War—the original having been buried with full military honours. His tactical genius ensured he lost the war—and his new leg. It was captured when Santa Anna beat a rapid retreat after Illinois infantrymen interrupted his lunch. It's still on display in the Illinois State Military Museum.

4. Lieutenant-General Sir Aylmer Hunter-Weston, World War 1 (1914–1918)

He "threw away men the way other men tossed away socks."
~ Les Carlyon

Picking the most idiotic British General of World War 1 is a tough call. That's like deciding who was the stupidest member of Oasis. What distinguishes Hunter-Weston from a crowded field is his complete disregard for the lives of his men.

Hunter Bunter, as he was unaffectionately known, was an eccentric. He enjoyed riding around on a motorcycle rather than a horse and loved inspecting latrines. All this might be endearing until you examine his military career. His resume included an inability to give clear orders or deviate from his plans, a lack of concern for the fate of his men, and ignoring sensible advice that might have reduced casualties and brought victory.

If you accept Einstein's definition of insanity (trying the same thing again and again with the expectation of different results), then his performance during the Gallipoli Campaign was insane. The French officers thought he'd lost his mind. He ordered his men to assault well-fortified Turkish positions, not once but four times. They had to run uphill in broad daylight (he rejected a night attack) without diversions or feints. Each time ended in disaster. He was about to try again until his senior commander finally intervened. During the campaign he rejected the Turkish offer of a temporary armistice to retrieve the wounded (so men died slowly in No-man's-land) and awarded a bravery medal to an officer who had three of his men shot for alleged cowardice.

Instead of a deserved court martial, they promoted Hunter-Weston to lieutenant general and put him in charge of an army corps. He was soon up to his old tricks. During the Battle of the Somme, he ignored advice to keep bombarding the enemy until the British infantry climbed out of their trenches, and ordered the guns to stop ten minutes before the charge. The Germans mowed his men down like summer grass.

After the war he received a knighthood from the King, presumably for services to the British mortuary industry.

5. General Maurice Gamelin, World War II (1939–1945)

"Generals always fight the last war,
especially if they have won it."
~ Anonymous

General Gamelin had been a decent staff officer in the First World War, but that was then. In 1939, as head of the French Army, he could not grasp that military strategy had changed and oversaw France's most humiliating ever defeat.

Gamelin stuck to rigid defence when the tank and the aircraft had made attack the name of the game. He might have caught Nazi Germany off guard when they invaded Poland, but he still kept French forces behind the Maginot Line. These sophisticated defensive fortresses were thought to be impregnable. Perhaps they were; the Germans simply went around them.

He was even told the date when the Germans would invade but did little to prepare for this, saying he would "await events." He didn't post adequate defences in the Ardennes Forest, thinking it too difficult for tanks to penetrate. This is, of course, where the enemy attacked.

There has been a rumour he was suffering from syphilis to explain his performance, though most historians now discount this theory. His mental incapacity was entirely down to incompetence.

6. General Francisco Solano, Lopez War of the Triple Alliance (1864–1870)

"We fought desperately because we loved our land insanely."
~ **Paraguayan war veteran**

Lopez was "a monster without parallel."
~ **George Thompson**

Lopez was responsible for the greatest proportionate loss of life in military history. Over eighty percent of adult Paraguayan males died in the War of the Triple Alliance, where Paraguay simultaneously took on Brazil, Uruguay, and Argentina.

Lopez also thought of himself as the "Napoleon of South America" and kept one hand inside his coat to imitate Bonaparte. He wasn't a great general but a deluded egomaniac who confused his own interests with those of his country, as Hitler was to do eighty years later. Lopez contemplated forcing the whole of Paraguay to commit

suicide when it looked like they might lose his precious war. Ruthless to the core, he had commanders who failed, tortured, and shot. If they fled, he would kill their families. Around one in three people were recruited as spies, ordered to shoot the other two if they were disloyal.

Lopez became more erratic as time went on. He saw no problem in indulging in orgies while trying to get the Catholic Church to make him a saint. (When twenty-three bishops refused his deification, he had them killed.) His mother was publicly flogged when she revealed he was illegitimate. Lopez wanted to execute her, but a Brazilian invasion saved her. He once had his wife place a portrait on his throne and made people bow to it. Ironically, because of his years of overindulgence, he couldn't run away from the enemy.

Thanks to the Napoleon of South America, Paraguay lost over fifty thousand square miles of land to her neighbours, while war devastated the rest of the country. Strangely, Paraguayans still regard El Fatso as a national hero.

7. General Hajienestis, Greco-Turkish War (1919–1922)

Perhaps appointing a madman as your commander wasn't the best idea. General Hajienestis had been a promising officer but in his mid-fifties he started going off his rocker. Lloyd George, the British prime minister, thought he was a "mental weakling." Unperturbed, the Greek government appointed him commander during Greece's war against Turkey.

Hajienestis immediately set up his HQ on a yacht in Smyrna Harbour so he didn't have to come into contact with his men. He wouldn't have been much good near the front as he believed his legs were made of sugar. When it became obvious that the Turks were winning the war, he developed another strategy for reality avoidance. He pretended he was dead and remained motionless for hours. He could now disclaim any responsibility for the disaster. His men were left in leaderless confusion and were routed by the Turks.

After the war, Hajienestis was shot for treason.

8. Major General Sir William Elphinstone, First Anglo-Afghan War (1839–1842)

"The greatest military idiot, of our day or any other day."
~ **George Macdonald Fraser**

"The most incompetent soldier who ever became a general."
~ **General William Nott**

He was already physically ailing when he reached newly conquered Afghanistan, suffering from a heart condition and gout. "Unfit for it in body and mind," he admitted. His last battle had been Waterloo, a mere thirty-seven years before. On the positive side, he had a good social background and played the right sports.

The British East India Company dominated India but wanted to extend its grip into neighbouring states. They forgot one of the golden rules of warfare. Never invade Afghanistan. They conquered it but, as other armies were to find out, this meant occupying Kabul while the Afghan male population took to the mountains and waged a pitiless guerrilla war.

When Elphinstone arrived, he knew that the British camp outside Kabul was vulnerable to attack but chose to do nothing. This was part of his hands-off style. Sporting events and concerts were organized instead. Perhaps with less cricket and Shakespeare, things might have been different.

The defeated Afghans were biding their time. When two British officials were murdered, Elphinstone once more did not act. This only encouraged the Afghans to launch a full-scale rebellion. Elphinstone chose to withdraw from Kabul to the nearest fort in India, but this meant marching through narrow passes in the middle of winter. The civilians would slow down the retreat. He therefore negotiated a truce with Afghan leader Akbar Khan, but this was trusting your enemy from a position of weakness. Sure enough, once the British left Kabul they were constantly attacked. Some of his subordinates urged turning back; but Elphinstone pressed on, refusing to hurry though speed was of the essence. It became a death march. Those who weren't killed by the Afghans, died of disease or committed suicide. Elphinstone made no attempt to direct operations, sitting silently on his horse, oblivious to the surrounding suffering. Of the sixteen thousand men, women, and children of the British East India Company, only one returned to Indian—a doctor whose reinforced hat spared his life from a sword blow. When asked where the British Army was, he replied, "I am the British Army."

Elphinstone died soon afterwards in captivity. It shattered the British reputation for invincibility in the Indian subcontinent.

9. General Alexander Samsonov, World War I (1914–1918)

"When [such a] mass suffers enormous losses; when they feel, as they will feel, that other and less costly means of achieving the same end might have been adopted, what will become of their morale?"
~ **G. F. R. Henderson**

Modern wars didn't last very long. It will be all over by Christmas, they said in the summer of 1914. But for the blunders of General Alexander Samsonov, they might have been right.

Germany had a terrible dilemma at the beginning of the First World War. Surrounded by enemies, they wondered how they could fight simultaneously on two fronts. The High Command developed a plan for a lightning march into France before the lumbering Russian war machine got going. Good in theory, but it soon unravelled. France proved a tough nut to crack, and the Russians mobilized in a matter of days; the Germans thought it would take weeks. With most of the German army fighting in the west, Eastern Germany now lay at the mercy of the Russian army.

Enter Samsonov. He was ordered to march rapidly into Germany with the Russian Second Army, accompanied by the First Army under General Rennenkampf. The Russians had a clear numerical superiority, so a rapid advance was essential. However, as historian Arthur Bloch wrote, "(Samsonov) had never been a front-line commander, but always a bureaucrat, serving in the rear." He moved more slowly than Rennenkampf and was soon three days adrift, leaving a dangerous gap between the two Russian armies. Worse, he and Rennenkampf were barely on speaking terms. They blamed each other for a defeat in the Russo- Japanese War nine years before. Even though their legendary fistfight never happened ("Yeah, do ya' want a piece Your Excellency"), the mutual loathing was real. There was now little attempt by the two sulking generals to coordinate.

Samsonov marched steadily on, unconcerned with the gap, or his stretched-out supply lines. He barely communicated with headquarters either. When he did, he transmitted wireless signal unencrypted, giving the Germans an exact idea of his movements. He might as well have sent them postcards. The Germans saw their only chance of victory and took it. Letting Samsonov pursue, they then encircled the rear of the First Army, cutting it off from Rennenkampf. Samsonov didn't realize he was being surrounded. He even detached a corps to attack Germans he thought were retreating. In fact, he was weakening his army and falling into their trap. When the truth dawned, he tried desperately to get Rennenkampf to come, but it was too late. Stuck in the Tannenberg Woods (which prevented them from fully using their artillery), only ten thousand of the one hundred and fifty thousand Russians escaped. Bloch wrote, "Samsonov had no idea where the Germans were or what he was supposed to do. He lost control of his forces and the Germans easily smashed his disorganized army... Samsonov gave up all hope for his army and rode off to the front to die in battle. Failing to accomplish even that, he committed suicide."

Russia never threatened German territory again, and the conflict bogged down into bloody trench warfare.

10. General Wilhelm Mauritz Klingspor, Finnish War (1808–1809)

He is euphemistically called a cautious commander. This is a polite word for a general who when the going gets tough usually gets going—in the other direction. He is immortalized in Johan Ludvig Runeberg's epic poem, *The Tales of Ensign Stal*, as the Supreme Idiot of the whole war.

Already in his sixties, he was a poor choice to defend Finland, then Swedish territory, from a Russian invasion. Instead of fighting them in the fjords, he decided on a tactical withdrawal (running away basically) up towards the Arctic Circle, leaving Helsinki at the mercy of the Russians.

His tiptoe to the tundra angered many younger staff officers who urged him to stand and fight. Klingspor didn't really like battles but reluctantly agreed. Preferring a desk to a cavalry horse he let his subordinates run things, which might explain why Sweden starting winning. But Cautious Klingy then failed to launch an all-out offensive despite the Swedes easily outnumbering the Russian army. This delay meant the Russians had time to reinforce. After defeat at the Battle of Oravais, Sweden ceded Finland to Russia. Klingspor went back to his desk.

Battle Fatigue:
History's Worst Military Mistakes

"Battles are won by slaughter and manoeuvre. The greater the general, the more he contributes in manoeuvre, the less he demands in slaughter."
~ **Winston Churchill**

1. The Charge of the Light Brigade, Crimean War (1854)

Perhaps the most infamous military screw-up of all time happened at the Battle of Balaclava, where a British and French force was fighting the Russians. During the battle, a strangely worded order told the British Light Brigade to charge the Russian guns. Which guns, though? The fact that two British commanders were not speaking to each other only added to the confusion. The Light Brigade charged the wrong ones into a well-prepared Russian defensive system (the Russians initially thought the British were drunk). Resplendent in their brilliant bright uniforms, they were massacred. "It was the most lethal costume party in history," wrote Sean Coghlan, as more than a third were killed or wounded.

2. Dien Bien Phu, Vietnam War (1954)

Underestimating your opponent is often the reason for military failure. The Battle of Dien Bien Phu is a classic example.

After World War II, France refused to grant Vietnam independence, resulting in a determined resistance movement called the Viet Minh. Like most Europeans, the French thought Asian troops inferior. Unlike the mighty and ever victorious French army, the Vietnamese could not fight a conventional battle; skulking around the jungles was their forte.

The French General, Henri Navarre, planned to lure the Viet Minh into a major confrontation by cutting off their supply routes. He had an airstrip built in Dien Bien Phu with eight strong points, each named after one of his mistresses. ("Arrogant; moi?") The French had occupied low ground, but they thought that wouldn't really matter. In fact, the Vietnamese proved to be disciplined and determined soldiers, not the ragbag guerrillas the French expected. Supplied with Chinese artillery, which the Viet Minh dragged through dense jungle and over mountains, they blasted the French forces out of Dien Bien Phu and out of Vietnam.

3. Battle of Hattin, The Crusades (1187)

Guy de Lusignan was the ruler of the crusader Kingdom of Jerusalem. During a war with Muslim forces in the Middle East, he decided a change of tactics was in order. He would attack the Muslims in open battle, whereas previously the Crusaders had successfully defended castles with good water supplies. Why? Guy had been accused of cowardice earlier and this might explain his recklessness. For a medieval knight, reputation was all. The result was the Kamikaze Crusader led his men against thirty thousand Muslims commanded by Saladin, the greatest general of the age. Desperate for water and already exhausted from the desert sun, Guy's army was destroyed.

When Pope Urban III heard the news, he died of shock.

4. Battle of the Teutoburg Forest, Roman-German Wars (9 ACE)

Never fight on your enemy's territory was a maxim that Roman general Publius Quinctilius Varus forgot with devastating consequences.

Varus had been a ruthless Governor of Syria, crucifying two thousand Jewish insurgents in a single day. He had the same approach as the new Governor of Germania, Rome's newly conquered Northern Province, but he proved to be no military commander. When attempting to put down a revolt near the River Rhine, Varus made a fatal error. He trusted Arminius, a captured son of a Germanic chief who had been brought up in Rome. Though outwardly loyal, he long nursed a desire for revenge and secretly plotted with German tribal leaders to destroy Varus' army. Varus ignored warnings about Arminius. Instead, he took his advice and marched three legions into the Teutoburg Forest where Arminius said a rebellion was taking place. It was a trap. The thick forest spread out the Roman Legions in a ten-mile trail allowing the Germans to pick them off in groups, rather than fighting them in open terrain. The three days of slaughter was intense; those Romans unlucky enough to be captured were crucified, burned or buried alive. It was the effective end of the Roman conquest of Germany.

Varus and most of his commanders committed suicide once the defeat became certain. According to the chronicler Suetonius, Emperor Augustus never recovered from the defeat. He suffered from depression and often called out, "Quinctilius Varus, give me back my Legions!"

5. Battle of Crecy, Hundred Years' War (1346)

Charging your own troops is not usually a wise decision, as Philip VI of France did against his English enemies. When his four thousand Genoese allies made no headway against the English long bowmen and retreated, he ordered his French knights to cut the Italians down. The English couldn't believe their luck and reigned arrows down on both the French and Genoese. About a third of Philip's army survived. The English lost fewer than a hundred.

6. Custer's Last Stand, Great Sioux War (1876)

"(Custer) was too hard on his men and horses. He changed his mind too often. He was always right. He never conferred enough with his officers. When he got a notion, we had to go."
~ **J. Horner, Corporal 7th Cavalry**

Another man guilty of underestimating his opponents, Custer failed to see Native Americans as worthy of respect.

When gold had been discovered in the Black Hills of South Dakota, the US Army was dispatched to "assist" Native Americans into reservations. Custer was an experienced Civil War cavalry officer, yet he made basic errors he would have avoided if fighting Confederates. He pursued a force of Lakota, Cheyenne, and Arapaho warriors; but he didn't wait for more US troops to arrive. Custer wanted the glory for himself and his Seventh Cavalry. Believing that the Native Americans were inferior, he didn't think numbers made a difference and expected them to run away when confronted by the US Cavalry. He even refused to take Gatling guns because they would embarrass him. Dividing his force into three weakened them and made defeat a certainty.

7. Suvla Bay Gallipoli, World War I (1915)

British General Stopford was well past his prime by the beginning of World War I. He had been valiantly pushing pens for King and Country for many years, but Field Marshall Kitchener insisted he was given a role in the attack on Gallipoli. Stopford, the younger son of the Earl of Courtown, was a stereotypical upper-class twit—and clueless about modern warfare. He had been an officer since 1871.

A British, Australian, and New Zealand force was pinned down by the Turks at Gallipoli; the only hope was a fresh landing on a different part of the coast so they ordered Stopford to attack the lightly defended beach of Suvla Bay. The way to Istanbul lay clear. When Stopford's force arrived on the beach, he took immediate action—and drank a cup of tea. He ordered his men to do likewise. Some of them even went for a swim. Good old Stoppers! By the time the ambling aristo was ready to attack, the Turks had reinforced their positions with two divisions. The British now faced a formidable opponent on higher ground. Needless to say, the British offensive was a hopeless failure. Stopford was fired a week later, but the damage had been done.

8. Battle of Karansebes, Austro-Turkish War (1788)

Sometimes battles are decided in the first few minutes of an encounter. Only once has a battle been lost before the enemy turned up.

During a campaign against the Turks, the Austrian forces had set up camp for the night. A boozy brawl developed. So far, so normal. Except one genius cried "Turci! Turci!" ("Turks! Turks!") — leading some to think the Turkish Army had launched a night attack. They ran through the camp but when officers shouted "Halt," some troops who could not speak German thought they said 'Allah." Full-scale panic now, made worse by the stampeding of horses (surely it must be the Turkish cavalry). Men shot at anything that moved. Many just fled. To add to the slapstick, the Austrian Emperor was knocked off his horse and into a stream. In the morning ten thousand men were killed or wounded.

And not a single Turk in sight.

143

9. Fort Douaumont Battle of Verdun, World War I (1916)

Douaumont was a key French fortification in their defensive line and one of the most formidable in the world. The problem was fewer than a hundred men garrisoned it. With a German attack imminent, General Chretien was ordered to supply Douaumont with reinforcements. He was about to go on leave but forgot to pass the message on to his replacement. The Battle of Verdun began shortly afterwards and the Germans easily took the fort. The French lost thousands trying to recapture it.

Note: the English translation of Chretien is cretin.

10. Battle of the Crater, American Civil War (1864)

"It was the saddest affair I have witnessed in this war."
~ **General Grant**

Petersburg was a vital railhead that supplied Richmond, the Confederate capital. Taking it might end the war, but the Confederacy tenaciously defended every inch of ground. The fighting bogged down into a stalemate by the summer of 1864 resembling the trench warfare of World War 1. To break the deadlock, Colonel Pleasants suggested filling a tunnel with explosives and blowing up a Confederate fort; the explosion would be so powerful Union forces could rush through the gap and on to Petersburg.

It was bold. It echoed the British attack on Messines Ridge fifty-three years later on the Western Front. Burnside reluctantly agreed. Normally everything Burnside touched turned to dross, but for once he wasn't to blame for the ensuing disaster. A division of African-American soldiers were to lead the assault but, less than twenty-four hours before the attack, General Meade got cold feet. He thought if things went wrong it would look as if they were sacrificing black troops needlessly. Burnside protested; the division had been rehearsing for days, but was overruled by General Grant. So a division of untrained white soldiers hastily replaced them.

The explosion was a success; Pleasants had been a mining engineer before the war. A thirty-foot hole was blasted under the Confederate lines and over 250 men were killed. But instead of taking immediate action, the Union troops, unclear about what to do next, waited for ten minutes and then climbed into the crater rather than around it. By now the Confederate forces had regrouped and could fire down into the crater at the sitting ducks below. The hole was so deep it trapped the Federals, and the soft, sandy soil made footholds difficult. No one had brought scaling ladders. Later the original African-American division was sent in (here Burnside was culpable) and met a similar fate, often killed in cold blood by Confederate troops after surrendering.

"Blood ran in the trenches all around," wrote a North Carolinian after the event. It was the end of Burnside's career, though Meade was mostly to blame. The Siege of Petersburg continued for another eight months.

Back to the Drawing Board: History Most Witless Weapons

1. Hughes H-4 Hercules or "Spruce Goose" World War II

"It is over five stories tall with a wingspan longer than a football field. That's more than a city block. Now, I put the sweat of my life into this thing. I have my reputation all rolled up in it and I have stated several times that if it's a failure I'll probably leave this country and never come back. And I mean it."
~ **Howard Hughes at the Senate hearing**

Designed by industrial tycoon Howard Hughes, the giant eight-engine flying boat would carry seven hundred and fifty troops the huge distances Americans needed to travel during the Second World War. The Spruce Goose, as it became known, had the largest wingspan in aviation history.

Made of wood to save on materials, the "flying lumberyard" was hugely expensive to develop and wasn't completed until 1947, two years after the war had finished. There was a Senate inquiry over the waste of public money, so Hughes demonstrated its aerial prowess. He flew only once, managing a mile at a breath-taking seventy feet above sea level. The project was effectively cancelled.

Spruce Goose? More like lame duck.

2. The Goliath, World War II

A case of ideas running ahead of technology: the Germans pioneered a remote-controlled tank fitted with explosives and named it The Goliath, Heidi. Despite the name, it was tiny and useless. The Goliath's top speed was six miles per hour and could be disabled by a direct hit or by cutting its control wires. More children's toy than weapon of war.

3. *H.M.S. Invincible,* World War I

This British battle cruiser is the most inappropriately named ship in naval history. *Invincible's* concept was "speed is the best protection" which really meant, "Let's get out of here quickly." Sure, it was quick, but it was so light that a hit from a German salvo broke its hull in two. *HMS Invincible* never posed a serious threat to enemy vessels, as its puny guns couldn't even fire at the same time. How did Britannia ever rule the waves?

4. Russian Dog Mines, World War II

From the nation that gave us Pavlov came these canine tank killers. They trained sniffer dogs to associate tanks with food; magnetic bombs were placed on their backs and then, hopefully, boom. The trouble was the dogs had been sniffing only Russian tanks. When they were released they went for their own side instead, causing a whole Russian tank division to retreat.

5. British Sticky Bombs, World War II

Grenade number seventy-four was intended for the British Home Guard to use against a Nazi invasion. Weighing five pounds, they were to be thrown at enemy tanks after removing the plastic seals. But it's hard to imagine Britain's part-time defence force of bakers and bank managers (nicknamed "Dad's Army") getting close enough to rampaging German Panzers. In experiments they often stuck to the soldiers' uniforms or failed to cling onto muddy tanks. Despite all this, they made two and a half million. Luckily, the German invasion never materialized.

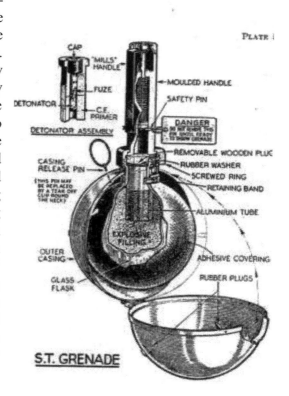

6. Japanese Balloon Bombs, World War II

By 1944 the war had turned against the Japanese and the US Air Force had made devastating attacks on their cities. Japan's military wanted to retaliate. As no plane could reach the US, they hit on balloon bombs. They sent almost ten thousand over but only one thousand made it, causing six deaths. That's a kill rate of 0.06 percent. Hardly terror from the skies.

7. The Bachem Natter, World War II

This German plane was almost a work of genius. Almost. Made of wood, it was one of the first vertically launched aircraft. During an enemy bombing raid, the Bachem Natter was meant to fire rockets at Allied aircraft until it ran out of fuel. The pilot would then parachute out of the Natter as it had no landing gear. The thrifty Germans had a separate parachute for the engine which could then be reused.

Unfortunately for its test pilot, the Bachem Nutter fell apart at high speed.

8. The Horse, in any Modern War

"I believe that the value of the horse and the opportunity for the horse in the future are likely to be as great as ever. Aeroplanes and tanks are only accessories to the men and the horse, and I feel sure that as time goes on you will find just as much use for the horse — the well-bred horse—as you have ever done in the past."
~ General Haig in 1926

The cavalry charge was still an important part of warfare until well into the nineteenth century. However, the invention of the machine gun and barbed wire should have ended any notion that the horse could still be used in battle. But the senior ranks in European armies were stocked with cavalry officers who were unwilling to believe their mounts were surplus to requirements. It was also a class thing. Most generals were from the aristocracy and viewed infantrymen with disdain; some of their officers hadn't gone to private schools! The tank was even worse; it raised the status of the scientist over the sportsman and put technology above elan.

During World War One, the British military leadership longed to settle the war in the traditional way: a full-tilt cavalry charge all the way to Berlin. But whenever they got their chance—at Cambrai, Amiens, and Vimy—there were predictably disastrous results.

The Poles have long been saddled with the last use of the horse on a modern battlefield. They were supposed to have charged a German tank regiment in World War II. It's a myth spread by Nazi propaganda.

9. The Ribaudo, Sixteenth Century

Invented by Antonio della Scala during the sixteenth century, the Ribaudo had 149 barrels, twelve of which could be fired at the same time. The problem was this comic contraption was too heavy and time-consuming to be effective on any battlefield. The machine gun had to wait for a more practical mind.

10. Mannlicher-Carcano Rifle, World War I and World II

Possibly the worst rifle in military history, the Mannlicher was notoriously inaccurate. Designed by an Austrian Count but used extensively by the Italian army, the long-suffering troops nicknamed the Mannlicher "the humanitarian rifle" because it always seemed to miss the enemy. This weapon undoubtedly contributed to Italy's below-par performance in both World Wars.

By the 1960s you could pick them up at gun shops for a couple of bucks. And that's exactly what Lee Harvey Oswald did before shooting Kennedy. Maybe this was the only time the Mannlicher ever hit anyone. Conspiracy theorists believe this is further proof that Oswald could not have been the assassin. They claim that when a top FBI marksman tested it at a hundred yards, the rifle consistently missed the target by up to five inches.

This Means War:
History's Most Ridiculous Conflicts

"When the war of giants is over the wars of pygmies begin"
~ Winston Churchill

1. The War of Jenkins' Ear, Britain v. Spain (1739–1748)

It incensed British public opinion when Robert Jenkins spoke before Parliament. A captain in the merchant navy, he appeared to have a slightly asymmetrical head. Spanish sailors cut off my ear, he complained, and they threatened to do the same to the King. The honor of Jenkins' ear was at stake, so Britain declared war. Years of inconclusive naval conflict followed, but Jenkins didn't do too badly. He became a celebrity on the London party circuit, displaying his now pickled ear in a box.

2. The Thirty Years' War and the Defenestration of Prague, Most of Europe (1618–1648)

The Thirty Years' War wasn't frivolous, but the spark that caused the war had a comic side. Three officials of Emperor Ferdinand were unceremoniously flung out of a window by rebellious Czech nobles. Instead of meeting a squashy end on the cobbled streets of Prague (it was a seventy-foot drop), they landed in a dung heap and survived. Angels had saved them, said the Emperor's supporters; luck replied his enemies. The ensuing war cost the lives of over eight million people.

Three Officials Flung Out a Window

3. The Pig War, Britain v. US (1859)

British Canada and the USA disputed the tiny island of San Juan. Relations worsened when an American farmer shot a pig belonging to an employee of the British Hudson Bay Company. The farmer offered inadequate compensation so both sides mobilized. At one point, four hundred and sixty-one Americans and fourteen cannons faced five British ships and two thousand troops.

Fortunately, cooler heads prevailed in London and Washington, and they reached a compromise. The pig was the only fatality.

4. The Pastry War, France v. Mexico (1838–1839)

This was a war between Mexico and France, not a food fight at a frat party.

Rioting Mexicans looted a French pastry shop in Mexico City. France demanded an astronomical sum in compensation. When it was not forthcoming, they sent a fleet to blockade Mexico.

The French care about food, you know.

5. The Football War, El Salvador v. Honduras (1969)

El Salvador and Honduras weren't getting on. There had been simmering tensions with Salvadorian immigrants in Honduras for years. When they played each other in a series of World Cup qualifiers, violence erupted between supporters at the end of the last game. El Salvador declared war on Honduras. Three thousand died. It's only a game, guys.

6. The War of the Bucket, Modena v. Bologna (1325)

When some Modenian soldiers filched a bucket, the citizens of Bologna were so outraged they declared war. The bucket was only made of wood but theft is theft. Thousands of casualties later, Modena still had the bucket and claimed victory.

If you're ever in Modena, you can still see it in the bell tower.

7. The Emu War, Australia v. a Bunch of Emus (1932)

By the 1930s the emu population had grown out of control in Australia's outback. To placate angry farmers, the government sent in crack troops to show the birds who was boss. But Emus can cut up rough, so the Aussies took no chances and brought machine guns—perhaps remembering Custer's mistake at the Battle of the Little Big Horn.

However, the emus proved fast and wily opponents. As chief emu slayer, Major Meredith, admitted, "If we had a military division with the bullet-carrying capacity of these birds it would face any army in the world... They can face machine guns with the invulnerability of tanks. They are like Zulus whom even Dum-Dum bullets could not stop." They killed very few emus before the Aussies gave up.

8. The War of the Golden Stool, Britain v. the Ashanti (1900)

The British are maestros of the pointless war, as they love invading other countries and ignoring their customs.

In 1900, the British kindly offered to take over the Ashanti's land and rule it for them. The Ashanti were not overly pleased, especially when the British representative Sir Frederick Hodgson wanted the Golden Stool for Queen Victoria to park her butt on. A graver insult could not have been imagined. The Golden Stool was the not just the symbol of Ashanti political authority but their most holy object. The Ashanti launched an assault on the British forces. Three thousand casualties later, the war ended. Though the Ashanti became part of the British Empire, Hodgson never got his stool.

9. The War of the Stray Dog, Greece v. Bulgaria (1925)

Scenario: Border tension between Greece and Bulgaria since World War 1. Act One: a Greek dog runs over the Bulgarian side and his master goes to retrieve him. Act Two: a dead Greek dog owner. Act Three: a pointless Greek invasion of Bulgaria which cost the lives of fifty men.

10. The Flagstaff War, Britain v. the Maoris (1845–1846)

Those Brits again. Hōne Heke, the Maori chief, thought the British were reneging on their treaty agreements and decided to teach them a lesson.

He chopped down the British flagstaff at Maiki Hill as a provocation. When they put it up again, he cut it down a second time. The Brits bought a new reinforced pole, but this still didn't prevent a Hone Heke hat trick. So, they built a blockhouse and put a considerable armed guard around the new flagstaff. Hōne Heke turned up with six hundred Maori warriors and made short work of the garrison and the pole.

The resulting war was bloody and indecisive, but the Brits had learned their lesson. They put a fifth flagstaff up in a different place, by Maori warriors, not the British government. It was now a symbol of reconciliation, not supremacy.

PART THREE:
The Things People Say

Withering Heights:
History's Nastiest Insults

**These quotes prove that politics
is the best contact sport of all.**

"He couldn't see a belt without hitting below it."
~ Margot Asquith, wife of Prime Minister Herbert Asquith
on his successor, David Lloyd George

*"He would kill his own mother just so that he could
use her skin to make a drum to beat his own praises."*
~ Margot Asquith on Winston Churchill

"A lamentably successful cross between a fox and a hog."
~ James G. Blaine,
senator, on Benjamin Franklin Butler, soldier

"He is a self-made man and worships his creator."
~ John Bright, British politician,
on Prime Minister Benjamin Disraeli

"A sheep in sheep's clothing."
~ Winston Churchill
on Labour Prime Minister Clement Attlee

"A modest man with much to be modest about."
~ Winston Churchill
on his long-suffering target, Clement Attlee

"He occasionally stumbled over the truth, but hastily picked himself up and hurried on as if nothing had happened."
~ Winston Churchill
on Stanley Baldwin, British prime minister

"A crafty and lecherous old hypocrite whose very statue seems to gloat on the wenches as they walk the State House yard."
~ William Cobbett, British writer,
on Benjamin Franklin

"Dear Randolph, utterly unspoiled by failure."
~ Noel Coward, playwright, on Randolph Churchill,
son of Winston Churchill

"If Gladstone fell into the Thames, that would be a misfortune, and if anybody pulled him out that, I suppose, would be a calamity."
~ Benjamin Disraeli on fellow
British Prime Minister William Gladstone

"He has committed every crime that does not require courage."
~ Benjamin Disraeli on Daniel O'Connell,
Irish nationalist politician

"If a traveller were informed that such a man was the leader of the House of Commons, he might begin to comprehend how the Egyptians worshiped an insect."
~ Benjamin Disraeli on
Lord John Russell, British prime minister

"His smile is like the silver fittings on a coffin."
~ **Benjamin Disraeli on British politician Robert Peel**

"I just won't get into a pissing contest with that skunk."
~ **Dwight D. Eisenhower on Senator Joseph McCarthy**

"Ronald Reagan doesn't dye his hair;
he's just prematurely orange."
~ **Gerald Ford on Ronald Reagan**

"People might cite George Bush as proof that you can be
totally impervious to the effects of Harvard and Yale education."
~ **Barney Frank on George W. Bush**

"Attila the Hen."
~ **Clement Freud, British MP on Margaret Thatcher**

"Garfield has shown that he is not possessed
of the backbone of an angleworm."
~ **Ulysses S. Grant on James A. Garfield**

"He has all the characteristics of a dog except loyalty."
~ **Sam Houston on Thomas Jefferson Green, politician**

"MacArthur is the type of man who thinks that when he gets to
heaven, God will step down from the great white throne
and bow him into His vacated seat."
~ **Harold Ickes talking about Douglas MacArthur**

"He's thin, boys.
He's thin as piss on a hot rock."
~ **Senator William E. Jenner on W. Averell Harriman**

"So dumb he can't fart and chew gum at the same time."
~ Lyndon Johnson on Gerald Ford

"He says he works out because it clears his mind.
Sometimes just a little too much."
~ Jay Leno on George W Bush

"His argument is as thin as the homeopathic soup
that was made by boiling the shadow
of a pigeon that had been starved to death."
~ Abraham Lincoln, on Stephen Douglas

"A retail mind in a wholesale business."
~ British Prime Minister David Lloyd George on
Conservative Prime Minister Neville Chamberlain

"Brilliant to the top of his boots."
~ David Lloyd George on Douglas Haig, British field marshal

"When they circumcised Herbert Samuel,
they threw away the wrong bit."
~ Lloyd George on Herbert Samuel, British politician

"The Right Honourable gentleman has sat so long on the fence
that the iron has entered his soul."
~ Lloyd George on Sir John Simon, British politician

"Like a cushion he always bore the impress
of the last man who had sat on him."
~ Lloyd George on Lord Derby
(also attributed to Douglas Haig)

"If he became convinced tomorrow that coming out for cannibalism would get him the votes he surely needs, he would begin fattening a missionary in the White House backyard come Wednesday."
~ H. L. Mencken talking about Franklin D. Roosevelt

"He slept more than any other president, whether by day or night. Nero fiddled, but Coolidge only snored."
~ H. L. Mencken on Calvin Coolidge

"He'll make a fine President. He was the best clerk who ever served under me."
~ Douglas MacArthur on President Dwight D. Eisenhower

"Shit in silk stockings."
~ Napoleon on Foreign Minister Talleyrand

"As he rose like a rocket, he fell like a stick."
~ Thomas Paine, British philosopher, about Edmund Burke, Anglo-Irish writer and politician

"How can they tell?"
~ Dorothy Parker on hearing that Calvin Coolidge had just died

"An empty suit that goes to funerals and plays golf."
~ Ross Perot talking about Dan Quayle

"Like rotten mackerel by moonlight, he shines and stinks."
~ John Randolph on Edward Livingston, Mayor of New York

"He was born with a silver foot in his mouth."
~ Ann Richards, Texas Governor, on George W. Bush

*"Washington couldn't tell a lie, Nixon couldn't tell the truth,
and Reagan couldn't tell the difference."*
~ Mort Sahl

*"He thinks himself deaf because he no longer
hears himself talked of."*
~ Charles Maurice de Talleyrand on
Vicomte de Chateaubriand

"He objected to ideas only when others had them."
~ A. J. P. Taylor, British historian,
on British foreign minister Ernest Bevin

"A triumph of the embalmer's art."
~ Gore Vidal on Ronald Reagan

*"With Sarah, do you get the feeling that in high school
she was voted least likely to read a book,
and the most likely to burn one?"*
~ Robin Williams on Sarah Palin

"He immatures with age."
~ British Prime Minister, Harold Wilson
on fellow politician Tony Benn

And some great retorts

"Sir, if you were my husband, I would poison your drink."
~Lady Nancy Astor

"Madam, if you were my wife, I would drink it."
~ Winston Churchill

"You will either die on the gallows or of a loathsome disease."
~ John Montagu

*"That depends on whether I embrace your principles
or your mistress."*
~ John Wilkes

"What do you think of Western civilization?"
a reporter once asked Mohandas Gandhi

"I think it would be a good idea," he replied.

In 1932 Babe Ruth was asked to justify why he received a
higher salary than President Herbert Hoover.
He retorted, *"Maybe so, but I had a better year than he did."*

Foot in Mouth:
History's Worst Political Bloopers

We shouldn't be too cruel. A politician is no more prone to mistakes than any other idiot. If microphones surround you all day, you will say some pretty dumbass things. The list shows how dull politics would be without constant media attention.

"We need laws that protect everyone. Men and women, straights and gays, regardless of sexual perversion, ah, persuasion."
~ **Rep. Bella Abzug speaking at**
a rally for the Equal Rights Amendment

"We do not want to destroy any people.
It is precisely because we have been advocating
co-existence that we have shed so much blood."
~ **Yasser Arafat**

*"Outside of the killings, Washington has one
of the lowest crime rates in the country."*
~ **Mayor Marion Barry, Washington, DC**

*"Those who survived the San Francisco earthquake said,
'Thank God, I'm still alive.' But, of course, those who died,
their lives will never be the same again."*
~ **Barbara Boxer, Senator**

*"Considering the dire circumstances that we have
in New Orleans, virtually a city that has been destroyed,
things are going relatively well."*
~ **Michael Brown, FEMA Director, after Hurricane Katrina**

*"Well on the manhood thing,
I'll put mine up against yours any time."*
~ **George H. W. Bush**

*"It's no exaggeration to say the undecideds
could go one way or the other."*
~ **George H. W. Bush**

*"For seven and a half years I've worked alongside
President Reagan. We've had triumphs. Made some mistakes.
We've had some sex... uh... setbacks."*
~ **George H. W. Bush**

"I want to make sure everybody who has a job wants a job."
~ **George H. W. Bush**

And in carrying on a fine family tradition, it's time for Dubya

"Our enemies are innovative and resourceful, and so are we. They never stop thinking about new ways to harm our country and our people, and neither do we."

"There's an old saying in Tennessee—I know it's in Texas, probably in Tennessee—that says, fool me once, shame on—shame on you. Fool me—you can't get fooled again."

"I know how hard it is for you to put food on your family."

"Families is where our nation finds hope, where wings take dream."

"Rarely is the questioned asked: Is our children learning?"

"We spent a lot of time talking about Africa, as we should. Africa is a nation that suffers from incredible disease."

"You teach a child to read,
and he or her will be able to pass a literacy test."
~ **George W. Bush**

"I have often wanted to drown my troubles,
but I can't get my wife to go swimming."
~ **Jimmy Carter**

"This is still the greatest
country in the world, if we
just steal our wills and
lose our minds."
~ **Bill Clinton**

"I'm not going to have
some reporters pawing
through our papers. We
are the president."
~ **Hillary Clinton**

"When a great many people are unable to find work,
unemployment results."
~ **Calvin Coolidge**

"Get this thing straight once and for all.
The policeman isn't there to create disorder.
The policeman is there to preserve disorder."
~ **Mayor Richard Daley of Chicago**

"I haven't committed a crime.
What I did was fail to comply with the law."
~ **David Dinkins, New York City Mayor**

"A billion here, a billion there.
Pretty soon it runs into real money."
~ **Everett Dirksen**

"The Internet is a gateway to get on the net."
~ **Bob Dole**

"I intend to open this country up to democracy,
and anyone who is against that, I will jail, I will crush."
~ **General Joao Baptista Figueiredo**

"Whenever I can I always watch
the Detroit Tigers on the radio."
~ **Gerald Ford**

"Many Americans don't like the simple things.
That's what they have against we conservatives."
~ **Barry Goldwater**

"The police are fully able to meet and compete with criminals."
~ **John F. Hylan, Mayor of New York**

"Nixon has been sitting in the White House
while George McGovern has been exposing himself
to the people of the United States."
~ **Frank Licht, governor of Rhode Island**

"If you can't lie, you'll never go anywhere."
~ Richard Nixon

"This is a great day for France!"
~ Richard Nixon, at Charles De Gaulle's funeral

"This is a discredited president."
~ Richard Nixon (he really meant 'precedent')

"But obviously, we've got to stand with our North Korean allies."
~ Sarah Palin

"Only dead fish go with the flow."
~ Sarah Palin

"All of 'em, any of 'em that have been in front of me over all these years" (on being asked which newspapers she reads).
~ Sarah Palin

"He who warned, uh, the British that they weren't gonna be takin' away our arms, uh, by ringing those bells, and um, makin' sure as he's riding his horse through town to send those warning shots and bells that we were going to be sure and we were going to be free, and we were going to be armed."
~ Sarah Palin, showing a wonderful grasp of history

Dan Quayle Deserves His Own Section.

*"Welcome to President Bush, Mrs. Bush,
and my fellow astronauts."*

*"We're going to have the best-educated
American people in the world."*

*"Mars is essentially in the same orbit. Mars is somewhat the
same distance from the sun, which is very important.
We have seen pictures where there are canals, we believe,
and water. If there is water, that means there is oxygen.
If oxygen, that means we can breathe."*

*"We have a firm commitment to NATO;
we are a 'part' of NATO.
We have a firm commitment to Europe.
We are a 'part' of Europe."*

*"The Holocaust was an obscene period in our nation's history.
I mean in this century's history.
But we all lived in this century. I didn't live in this century."*

*"Quite frankly, teachers are the only profession
that teach our children."*

*"It isn't pollution that's harming the environment.
It's the impurities in our air and water that are doing it."*

"It is wonderful to be here in the great state of Chicago."

"I love California; I practically grew up in Phoenix."

*"Desert Storm was a stirring victory
for the forces of aggression and lawlessness."*

*"Republicans understand the importance
of bondage between a mother and child."*

*"We are ready for any unforeseen event
that may or may not occur."*

"If we don't succeed, we run the risk of failure."

*"What a waste it is to lose one's mind,
or not to have a mind.
How true that is."*

"I stand by all my misstatements."

~ Dan Quayle

"I didn't go down there with any plan for the Americas, or anything. I went down there to find out from them and their views. You'd be surprised. They're all individual countries."
~ **Ronald Reagan after his visiting Latin America**

"The United States has much to offer the Third World War."
~ **Ronald Reagan (who said this eight times in the same speech)**

"Now we are trying to get unemployment to go up and I think we're going to succeed."
~ **Ronald Reagan**

"The streets are safe in Philadelphia. It's only the people who make them unsafe."
~ **Frank Rizzo, Mayor of Philadelphia**

"Half the lies our opponents tell about us aren't true."
~ **Boyle Roche, eighteenth century Irish politician**

"I am honoured today to begin my first term
as the Governor of Baltimore—that is Maryland."
~ **William Donald Schaefer**

"The President has kept all the promises
he intended to keep."
~ **George Stephanopoulos**

Trumpisms: The Wisdom of Donald Trump

"The symptoms of narcissistic personality disorder include grandiose sense of importance, preoccupation with unlimited success, belief that one is special and unique, exploitative of others, lack of empathy, arrogance, and jealousy of others."
~ **Dr John M. Grohol**

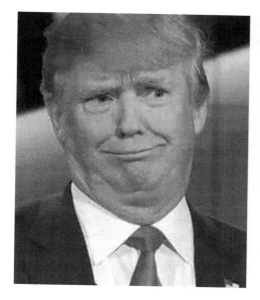

One thing you can say about President Trump is what you see is what you get. Sadly, what you get is a pompous, ignorant narcissist who in a tsunami of tweets and rallies to the faithful, has lied, belittled, and paraded his ignorance. Here are just a few.

"I could stand in the middle of Fifth Avenue and shoot people and I wouldn't lose voters."

"That makes me smart" on not paying taxes."

"I'm going to have to scare the Pope."

"My wife says I'm the biggest star in the world. But she might just be saying that because she's intelligent."

175

"It's very close to my heart because I was down there, and I watched our police and our firemen down at 7/11, down at the World Trade Centre right after it came down..."
~ **Trump wasn't there at the time.**

"The beauty of me is that I'm very rich."

It's freezing and snowing in New York—we need global warming!"

"I've said if Ivanka weren't my daughter, perhaps I'd be dating her."

"They had a person who was extremely proud that a number of the women had become doctors. And I wasn't interested."
~ **Trump on the Miss America pageant.**

"I know nothing about the inner workings of Russia."

"When Mexico sends its people, they're not sending their best. ...They're sending people that have lots of problems, and they're bringing those problems with us. They're bringing drugs. They're bringing crime. They're rapists."

"Look at that face! Would anyone vote for that? Can you imagine that, the face of our next president? I mean, she's a woman, and I'm not supposed to say bad things, but really, folks, come on. Are we serious?"
~ **Trump's description of Carly Fiorina.**

"I'm a very stable genius."

"Nambia's (sic) health system is increasingly self-sufficient."

"The FAKE NEWS media (failing @nytimes, @NBCNews, @ABC, @CBS, @CNN) is not my enemy; it is the enemy of the American People!"

"The Democrats are politicising the coronavirus...They're politicising it. One of my people came up to me and said: 'Mr President, they tried to beat you on Russia, Russia, Russia.' That did not work out too well. They could not do it. They tried the impeachment hoax. This is their new hoax."

"I can't be doing so badly, because I'm president, and you're not. You know. Say hello to everybody, OK?" ~ To a journalist after a difficult interview.

"Maybe at some point, we'll have to take those rules on, because, for the good of the nation, things are going to have to be different."
~ Trump on getting rid of the checks and balances system.

"I just fired the head of the FBI. He was crazy, a real nut job..."

"There were fine people on both sides."
~ Trump commenting on the Charlottesville rally where neo-Nazis, white supremacists, and Klansmen clashed with anti-racist protestors, as Trump partially blames anti-racist protestors for the murder of Heather Heyer.

"[I've] only been a politician for a short period of time. How am I doing? Am I doing okay? I'm president. Heh! Hey, I'm president!" ~ On passing the Health Care Bill to repeal Obamacare through the House of Representatives–it was later blocked in the Senate.

"There is a cooling and there is a heating, and I mean, look: It used to not be climate change. It used to be global warming... That wasn't working too well, because it was getting too cold all over the place."

"Never has there been a president, with few exceptions... who has passed more legislation, done more things," said Trump after only five months in office, without having passed a single major piece of legislation.

"Like when you guys put somebody in the car and you're protecting their head, you know, the way you put their hand over? Like, don't hit their head, and they've just killed somebody—don't hit their head. I said you can take the hand away, OK?" (Talking to NYPD officers.)

"I love golf, but if I were in the White House, I don't think I'd ever see Turnberry again. I don't think I'd ever see Doral again... I don't ever think I'd see anything. I just want to stay in the White House and work my ass off."

"Black guys counting my money! I hate it. The only kind of people I want counting my money are short guys that wear yarmulkes every day... I think that the guy is lazy. And it's probably not his fault, because laziness is a trait in blacks. It really is; I believe that. It's not anything they can control." Trump at first denied he had said this and then later admitted he probably did.

"I've got to use some Tic Tacs, just in case I start kissing her. You know I'm automatically attracted to beautiful—I just start kissing them. It's like a magnet. Just kiss. I don't even wait. And when you're a star, they let you do it. You can do anything... Grab them by the pussy. You can do anything."

Infamous Last Words:
History's Funniest Parting Shots

We can't select the time of our exit, so last words are undignified. The ones that sound well prepared are sentimental or pompous, like General Nathan Hale's "I only regret that I have one life to lose for my country." President Eisenhower sounded like he was delivering an Oscar speech when he said, "I've always loved my wife, my children, and my grandchildren, and I've always loved my country. I want to go. God, take me." The list below says far more about the human condition.

"Am I dying or is this my birthday?"
~ Lady Astor, Anglo-American Politician (1879 –1964)

She spoke her last words when, on her deathbed, she momentarily awoke to find herself surrounded by her entire family.

"Jefferson still survives."
~ John Adams, US President (1735–1826)

John Adams was a bitter old man. He'd been the only president not to be re-elected to date. His political party, the Federalists, had collapsed; and worst of all, his political rival, Thomas Jefferson, had enjoyed a brilliantly successful career. Jefferson had beaten Adams in the 1800 elections and his party, the Democratic Republicans, now dominated the political landscape. Adams came to hate Jefferson with a passion. Even on his deathbed he thought Jefferson had triumphed once again and outlived him. Unfortunately, Jefferson had passed away a few hours earlier, but with communications being so slow, Adams died ignorant of his one triumph.

"Go away; I'm all right."
~ HG Wells, British Science Fiction Writer
and Historian (1866–1946)

For a man famed for his ability to write about the future, H. G. Wells was inept at predicting his own.

"Waiting, are they?
Waiting, are they?
Well, let 'em wait."
~ Ethan Allen, U.S. General (1838–1889)

Allen's last words were a deathbed response to a doctor who attempted to comfort him by saying, "General, I fear the angels are waiting for you."

"God damn the whole world and everyone in it."
**~ W.C. Fields,
US Comedian
(1880–1946)**

A wonderfully honest parting shot from the old curmudgeon.

Fields was suffering from a stomach haemorrhage brought on by years of bad living and went out with typical misanthropy.

"I am still alive."
**~ Caligula, Roman
Emperor (12-41 ACE)**

Uttered after assassins had just stabbed the Roman tyrant. He then died.

"I think I could eat one of Bellamy's veal pies."
~ William Pitt the Younger, British prime minister (1759-1806)

Sadly, Mr. Pitt didn't have time to eat Bellamy's famous savouries—nor anything else for that matter.

"Nonsense, they couldn't hit an elephant at this distance."
~ General John Sedgwick, American Civil War Commander (1813–1864)

General Sedgwick was standing on the parapet at the Battle of the Wilderness. A subordinate warned him of the danger, but Sedgwick brushed aside any suggestion that the enemy might shoot him. Then the enemy shot him.

"Now I'm oiled, keep me from the rats."
~ Pietro Aretino, Italian Satirist (1492-1556)

Renaissance satirist Aretino laughed so hard at one of the Duke of Urbino's jokes he had a stroke. Aretino revived during the last rites to utter this valediction.

*"Last words are
for fools
who haven't
said enough."*
~ **Karl Marx, German
founder of Communism
(1818–1883)**

When asked if he had any last words, Marx gave this reply. Judging by the list, he was probably right.

PART FOUR:
Myths and Miscellaneous:
Everyday Idiocy

What a Way to Go: History's Silliest Deaths

*"The difference between tragedy and comedy
is that one's own death is tragic;
it is other people's that are comic."*
~ Anonymous

Edward II, English King (1284–1327)

Edward II had become so unpopular that a group of nobles had him murdered. To avoid any incriminating marks, they shoved a red-hot poker up his rectum. Though this was hardly a discreet method of execution, they probably heard his screams all the way to Moscow.

Aeschylus, Ancient Greek Playwright (523–456 BCE)

Known for writing tragedies, his death raises more laughs than his plays ever did. While out walking, he was hit on the head by a tortoise, accidentally dropped by a passing eagle. The tortoise was travelling so fast when it hit poor Aeschylus' balding pate, it killed the playwright immediately.

Oliver Goldsmith, Irish Poet and Playwright (1730–1774)

Convinced of the restorative powers of antimony, a quack medicine of the eighteenth century, Goldsmith showed its effectiveness by drinking a glass. He died shortly afterwards.

Li Po, Chinese Poet (701–762 ACE)

One of China's greatest classical poets, Li Po was a terrible boozer. Eventually drink was to prove his downfall. Out one night with the boys, he took a boat trip, despite already being the worse for wear. When he reached the middle of the lake, he noticed the moon reflected in the water, so Li Po bent over the side of the boat and tried to kiss its reflection. Result: one drowned Chinese classical poet.

Francis Bacon, English Politician and Scientific Philosopher (1561–1626)

Walking in a snowstorm, Bacon wondered whether freezing a dead animal could preserve it for longer. So, he bought a dead chicken and stuffed it with ice. But Bacon became so cold he caught a chill which developed into pneumonia. His death meant we had to wait three centuries before the invention of the refrigerator.

Raphael, Italian Artist (1483–1520)

Raphael was renowned for painting gentle, tranquil pictures, particularly of the Madonna. In his private life, he was a sixteenth-century party animal, and something of a ladies' man. After what today's tabloids would describe as a romp, the exhausted Renaissance love machine caught a fever. According to biographer Vasari, Raphael was ashamed to tell the doctor the true cause of his illness and was prescribed the wrong medicine.

The Great Lafayette, German Magician (1871–1911)

Otherwise known as Sigmund Neuberger, this German magician was famous for his lavish and spectacular shows. During a performance in Scotland, he was killed when a lamp fell on his head. The Great Lafayette had already treated the audience to a disappearing goat, several birds, a trick involving a fake lion almost eating his assistant, and a trumpet fanfare. When the lamp hit the uber-illusionist, he was taking his final bow. Many of the audience thought it was part of the act and wildly applauded, particularly when the stage burst into flames.

Eleven people were killed in the blaze, including several members of the orchestra and a midget. The Great Lafayette was thought to have died on stage until a body was discovered in the basement with his trademark rings. It transpired that the first corpse was one of Lafayette's doubles he used for his illusions.

The Great Lafayette was buried in a lavish funeral along with his beloved dog Beauty. Houdini sent Beauty a wreath.

Rasputin, Russian Mystic and Monk (1869–1916)

This faith healer ingratiated himself with the Russian royal family by helping to relieve the Crown Prince's haemophilia. But he was a man with a dubious reputation, known as a drinker and womanizer. As his influence grew in court, so did the aristocracy's resentment. Many of them thought this peasant was making the Tsar and Tsarina look like fools. Prince Felix Yusupov and some friends hatched a murder plot. They invited Rasputin for a meal and then given huge amounts of cyanide, but this didn't seem to have any effect so his assassins shot him. Incredibly, when Yusupov returned for his coat, Rasputin opened his eyes and tried to strangle him. Perhaps his murderers started to believe the legend that Rasputin had magic powers. They shot him a further three times and then bound him and threw him in the icy Neva River. Later the autopsy revealed his arms were in an upright position, as if he was trying to fight his way through the ice.

It shows that you can't keep a bad man down.

Tycho Brahe, Danish Astronomer (1546–1601)

During a long dinner party, the famous astronomer realized he needed to relieve himself. Not wishing to offend anyone, he thought he should remain seated until the dinner was over. However, the wine flowed and Brahe became increasingly desperate and burst his bladder. An infection set in and eleven days later he died.

Nicola Coviello, Musician (1867–1913)

Coviello died of jazz music—an unusual complaint. The great classical musician was visiting relatives in America, who wanted to show him some of its sights and sounds. However, Coviello took an immediate dislike to jazz.

"This isn't music!" he exclaimed, and then promptly died of what they later put down to "a strain on the heart."

He's Called What?
History's Most Ridiculous Names

Some statesmen's names have suited their brilliant political careers. Abraham gave Lincoln the air of a Biblical prophet. Nelson, associated with bravery since Admiral Nelson, fitted Mandela. The situation works in reverse: some politicians have been cursed with names so comical they seem predestined to fail.

King Zog, Albanian King (1928–1939)

Famous for having the strangest name in history, King Zog was born plain Ahmed Bey Zogu, a tribal leader who muscled his way to the power in 1925. He felt a royal title would give his rule an air of respectability.

Instead, it made him sound like the bad guy from an old Flash Gordon movie.

Rev. Canaan Banana, Zimbabwean President (1980–1987)

He was little more than a figurehead, as the real power lay with the sinister Prime Minister, Robert Mugabe. Mugabe kicked Banana out of office in 1987 and became president. The Reverend was later found guilty of sodomy and defrocked.

Gheorghe Gheorghiu-Dej, Romanian Dictator (1948–1965)

It would have been some task to write a campaign song for the man. Few words rhyme with Gheorghiu Dej, even in Romanian. "Gheorghe Boy" was an unrepentant Stalinist who gave Romania seventeen miserable years of misrule.

Wim Kok, Dutch Prime Minister (1994–2002)

Not especially funny in Holland, but always got a laugh in the English- speaking world.

Marmaduke Grove, Chilean President (1935)

Bravely went into public life, despite his name, and seized power in 1935. Grove's regime lasted ten days.

Lon Nol, Cambodian President (1970–1975)

Lon Nol ineffectively ran Cambodia before the horrors of the Khmer Rouge. This palindromic premiere enjoys the rare political distinction of having a last name that's the same as his first name, only spelt backwards. U Nu, former leader of Burma, is also in this exclusive club though he doesn't have as many letters. Go and get a longer name U if you want to make this list.

Koci Xoxe, Albanian Minister of the Interior (1944–1949)

After Zog, the Albanians gamely continued their tradition of bizarrely monikored politicians, with this effort from the early years of communist rule. Xoxe (pronounced I don't have the foggiest) spent much of the time having people shot until, after five years, it was his turn before the firing squad.

King Carol II, Romanian King (1930–1940)

Isn't that a girl's name? Possibly his parents wanted to toughen him up. Like Johnny Cash's *Boy Named Sue*. Perhaps that's why Carol joined forces with Hitler during World War II. There was nothing feminine about that. Trouble was, Romania was hopelessly unprepared and easily conquered by the Soviet Union. Oh Carol.

Millard Fillmore, President (1850–1853)

"(The students would ask) who is Fillmore? What's he done? Where did he come from? And then my name would, I fear, give them an excellent opportunity to make jokes at my expense." ~ **Millard Fillmore, on the reasons why he refused an honorary Oxford degree**

Knowing student humour, he was wise to stay away.

Despite being aware

of his ridiculous name,

he called his son...

Millard Fillmore.

William Rufus De Vane King, Vice President (1853)

He only lasted six weeks before dying of consumption. Why the Democrats nominated a man not long for this world remains a mystery. King, incidentally, is the only vice president that has ever had an affair with a US president (James Buchanan if you want to know, though neither were in office at the time).

Still Doing the Rounds:
History's Greatest Myths

George Washington Chopped Down a Cherry Tree.

We should blame Mason Locke Weems, a writer of sentimental fiction, who penned the *Life of George Washington: with Curious Anecdotes, Equally Honourable to Himself and his Young Countrymen*. With such a snappy title, it sold by the bucketful.

The book though was full of errors. The most famous being the passage when young George is asked by his father whether he'd cut down a cherry tree on their estate. Rather than do what most self-respecting boys would and blame his brother, George replied, "I can't tell a lie Pa; I did cut it with my hatchet." Pa then embraced George and said he was glad his son cut down the tree, because he'd proved his honesty. "Such an act of heroism... is more worth than a thousand trees..." said the sobbing Washington Senior.

A story to warm the cockles of your heart—and not a word of it is true.

The Pilgrim Fathers and Thanksgiving

Never has so much nonsense been told to so many about so few. It's hard to know where to start to unpick. The Pilgrim Fathers were not fleeing religious persecution in England; they had already done that by moving to the more religiously tolerant Holland. They left the Netherlands, via Plymouth, because they didn't want their children to become assimilated into Dutch culture. They didn't dress in black with buckled shoes (that was the Quakers of Pennsylvania), nor did they call themselves Pilgrims but Saints. They weren't Puritans but Separatists, a stricter religious sect whose most famous member was

Oliver Cromwell. They didn't land on Plymouth Rock, which was navigationally risky, but further inland. They weren't the first English settlers in the New World; Virginia had been up and running for over a decade. For years, Southerners resented Thanksgiving as a "Yankee Festival."

Squanto (called Tisquantum), the Native American who saved them from starvation, wasn't someone who had just emerged from the wilderness, but a man who had lived in England and spoke fluent English. How else would these monolinguistic colonizers communicate with him?

This story of triumph over adversity has all the validity of Santa Claus and his elves.

Nostradamus' Predictions Were True.

Isn't he the French guy who lived hundreds of years ago and predicted Kennedy's assassination? And Hitler's rise? And the 9/11 attacks? No, he's the French guy who lived hundreds of years ago whose predictions were so vague almost anything can be read into them. Neither did he forecast the end of the world correctly, the date of his own death, nor the year of his exhumation.

Admittedly, Nostradamus hasn't been helped by people fabricating his work. The Nazis inserted the word Hitler instead of Hister into one of his quatrains. Hister was the old word for the Danube from where Nostradamus had written that a great leader would emerge. The Nazis then claimed the prophet had predicted the Fuhrer's rise to power.

His 9/11 prediction also seems scarily accurate:

> *"In the year of the new century and nine months, from the sky will come a great King of Terror..? The sky will burn at forty-five degrees. Fire approaches the great new city...*
>
> *In the city of York there will be a great collapse, two twin brothers torn apart by chaos while the fortress falls the great leader will succumb; third big war will begin when the big city is burning."*

The only problem is he didn't write it. Just like that couple getting their photo taken on top of the World Trade Centre as the plane careered towards them; it's a forgery produced after the event.

Thomas Crapper and the Modern Flush Toilet

He is an indoor plumbing legend. Yet Thomas Crapper didn't invent the modern toilet which he catchily named "The Silent Valveless Water Waste Preventer." Crapper bought the design from a man called Albert Giblin. Paying a trifling sum for the patent, the sultan of sanitation stole all the glory and died a rich man—and a household name.

How different the English vernacular would be if Crapper hadn't bought up the rights, or is that just a load of Giblin?

Benjamin Franklin and that Kite

History books tell us how Benjamin Franklin and his young son discovered the electrical properties of lightning by flying a kite in a storm. The problem was no eighteenth-century kite could have got high enough in the sky. Franklin himself was suspiciously vague on the details and the accounts he gave contradict each other. No witnesses were around either. The science was valid, but the episode seems to have come from his vivid imagination.

Pope Joan I, the Only Female Pontiff

This medieval legend is often repeated, with several websites and societies dedicated to the memory of the only female pope. The trouble was she never existed. The story goes something like this: Pope "John" was elected in 855 ACE and everything seemed normal for the next three years until Her Holiness was taken ill during a papal procession. On closer inspection it transpired the Pope was in labor and gave birth to a baby boy. The populace was so incensed about this deception they stoned Joan/ John to death. Other versions have Joan dying of childbirth or being sent to a nunnery while her son became a bishop. They then put holes in the seats of subsequent Popes to make sure they had the right genitalia.

The truth is more prosaic. Benedict III died in 855 and was succeeded by Leo IV. Both were male.

Catherine the Great Wasn't Killed by a Horse.

It's an old standby for history teachers looking for a few classroom giggles. Catherine the Great, Russia's ruler in the late eighteenth century, is supposed to have been fatally injured while attempting congress with a four-legged friend. In fact, she died of a stroke while on a commode. Catherine's many enemies spread the rumour to discredit her. The Queen's sexual voracity wasn't a legend, but her taste was entirely for men.

German almost Supplanted English as the Official Language of the United States.

When the US had achieved independence from Britain, its Constitutional Convention contemplated making German its official language. This was because many Americans were so antagonistic to their former rulers, anything that smacked of the old regime needed to be changed. According to one report, English only defeated German by one vote.

Untrue, over ninety percent of Americans were of British descent and for practical reasons saw no need to learn another language. The debate never occurred, though the House of Representatives did briefly consider publishing laws in English *and* German to help new immigrants. They overwhelmingly rejected the proposal.

"Ring a Ring o' Roses" is about the Black Death.

This has been repeated so often that it is widely believed and rarely questioned. The children's nursery rhyme, "Ring a Ring o' Roses," was about the bubonic plague. The "ring" round the "roses" supposedly refers to the red, round rash that appeared on people's arms—the first symptom of the plague. The "pocketful of posies"

are the flowers that people believed provided protection from the disease. "Ashes, ashes we all fall down" refers to the final stages of the plague when sufferers often sneezed and then died.

It all seems to fit, but on closer examination the whole theory falls apart. The Black Death occurred in 1347, but the first written evidence for the rhyme dates from 1881. Folklorists had been collecting nursery rhymes for centuries, yet this one wasn't written down for over five hundred years! Also, if the rhyme originates from the plague, why isn't it in Middle English? And there are lots of different versions, all of them occurring from the same time. Two examples are,

Round the ring o' roses,
Pots full of posies,
The one stoops the last
Shall tell whom she loves the best

Round the ring of roses,
A bottle full of posies,
All the girls in our town
Ring for little Josie.

None of these can be linked to the Black Death. The connection between the famous rhyme and the bubonic plague is a coincidence.

Caligula Made his Horse a Consul.

According to legend, the Roman Emperor Caligula promoted his horse to the rank of consul. This has often been cited as proof of his mental derangement. Caligula wasn't that mad. The story springs from a misunderstanding of a joke Caligula made. When he said he'd rather make his horse a consul, he was being ironic. It was a jibe aimed at the politicians of the time who he thought useless.

Pointless Pursuits: History's Worst Sports

1. Shin Kicking (Britain)

The British have a knack of inventing sports: football, cricket, tennis, rugby. The trouble is when they teach them to the world; the world has the temerity to beat them. They should let us win now and again as a thank you.

Fortunately, not all British sports have attracted universal attention and so Britain can still claim pre-eminence in several. One of them is shin-kicking, particularly popular in the Cotswolds. The rules are simple. You kick your opponent's shins until he gives up, but if both of you want to endure incredible pain, the winner is the one who lands the most kicks. Padding is now used, but at one time it was bare shins and steel-toed boots. Contestants used to build up their pain threshold by hitting themselves with hammers.

No wonder it never spread like football.

2. Cruel Cat Sports (Europe)

Cats are one of the most adorable creatures on Earth. We spend billions yearly pampering our feline friends. So why were medieval people so cruel to them? Historians think perhaps their association with witches made them synonymous with evil. Another reason is more prosaic. There were sometimes too many of them in a town, and cat games were a form of pest control. Around Europe, they devised horrible sports which were glorified acts of torture. Perhaps the nastiest was in Bologna, where a man had his hands tied behind his back and tried to bite the head off a cat, whose claws had been deliberately sharpened. To the credit of some university students, they tried to get it banned. The most famous cat game was at Ieper in Belgium, largely because a facsimile continues to this day. They still throw stuffed cats off the roof of the Cloth Hall on Cat Wednesday during Lent. However, until in 1817, they were live ones. The last contestant fortunately survived and scampered away. Attitudes were changing by then: they saw witchcraft as just "so medieval", animal welfare societies were forming and cats received a boost during the French Revolution as being regarded as the people's pets, unlike dogs who were still associated with the aristocracy.

3. Goosepulling (Spain)

Invented in Spain in the 12th century, it spread across Western Europe and eventually to North America. In this squalid little activity, they attached a greased goose to a pole and a horseman tried to pull its head off as he rode past. This sport continues to this day in Germany and the Low Countries on Shrove Monday or Tuesday with one concession to animal rights. The goose is already dead.

4. Solo Synchronized Swimming (Global)

This isn't a wind-up. It was an Olympic event between 1984and 1992. Instead of the graceful and perfectly synchronized water ballet of the team event, competitors had to synch by themselves. Eventually, it was dropped from the Olympics out of sheer silliness.

5. Finch Sport or Vinkensport (Belgium)

This Belgium sport is relatively humane compared to the other animal games. Vinkensport is on the list because it's so dull. The 'finchers', or 'vinkeniers', sit by a caged bird for an hour tallying the number of times it tweets. The finches are selectively bred like racehorses and fed a high-protein diet during the year. Being Belgian, the Flemish and Wallonian vinkeniers maintain that their own birds sing in either Flemish or French, respectively.

If you want to know more about this fascinating subject, there is the Museum of Vinkensport in Hulste. Book early to avoid disappointment.

6. Cheese Rolling (Britain)

This event dates back centuries and its exact origins are unknown, possibly its roots lie in the pre-Roman era. The Cooper's Hill Cheese-Rolling and Wake is held annually near Gloucester, England, and attracts competitors from all over the world. A large Double Gloucester cheese is given a one-second start down the hill and competitors try to catch it. If no one does (and it can reach 70 miles per hour), the first person over the line is the winner. The speed and weight of the cheese can cause spectators to be injured, so they introduced a foam replica in 2013, much to the disgust of traditionalists.

7. Naumachia or Mock Naval Battles (Ancient Rome)

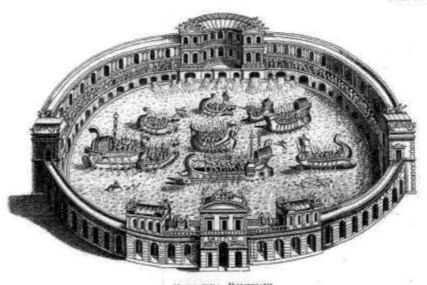

NAUMACHIA DOMITIANI.

Ah, the Romans! The most advanced civilisation of the ancient world: the aqueducts, the roads, central heating. But then there are the gladiatorial games. The brutality of the combat has been exaggerated; most of the time no one was killed, as they were expensive to train. But people still died for the entertainment of the crowd who thought this a great way to spend an afternoon.

But the gladiator contests were eclipsed by something far more elaborate and equally deadly. The Naumachia or Mock Naval Battles. These spectacles involved recreating naval sea battles, sometimes on man-made lakes. Suetonius describes one event under Emperor Claudius which used nine thousand prisoners. They were not free-for-alls but carefully planned to resemble historical battles. It's like digging up Central Park and filling it with water to stage Midway. As most of the participants were slaves (though a few nutters volunteered) they were not overly concerned with health and safety. Hundreds died. The famous phrase, "We who are about to die salute you" isn't from gladiator fights but Naumachia.

8. Jack-an-apes (Medieval Europe)

In Medieval Europe, when humans had to endure gruesome tortures, it's not surprising how badly animals were treated. Bulls fought dogs, dogs fought bears, and cocks clawed each other to death. They thought this was all fun.

One particularly nasty game was called jack-an-apes. They strapped a monkey on the back of a horse which then ran around a ring pursued by a pack of savage hounds. One witness wrote that "It is wonderful to see the horse galloping along, kicking up the ground and champing at the bit, with the monkey holding tightly to the saddle, and crying out frequently when he is bitten by the dogs."

9. Fox Tossing or 'Fuchsprellen' (Central Europe)

Popular in Central Europe in the early modern period, especially among the upper-classes, two people would catapult a fox into the air using a sheet. Wildcats, wolves and hares were also used. If any animals turned on their assailants, they were killed. Wildcats, in particular, didn't play the game and, as one contemporary wrote, "do not give a pleasing kind of sport, for if they cannot bury their claws and teeth in the faces or legs of the tossers, they cling to the tossing-slings for dear life, and it is next to impossible to give one of these animals a skilful toss." Spoilsports.

10. Dwarf tossing (Australia)

This sport (and I use the term in its loosest sense) was popular in Australia and the US in the 1980s, though it's now banned by several states. The venues are usually bars and pubs where the thrower attempts to toss a person suffering from dwarfism as far as possible. A variation is dwarf bowling, which uses skateboards and ten-pin bowls.

And we look down on medieval people as barbaric.

They Used to Eat That?
History's Worst Dishes

1. Dormice (Ancient Rome)

The Romans loved nothing more than tucking into a dormouse, but not the common-or-garden variety. No, the connoisseur ate glires, a larger, juicier specimen regarded as a delicacy. They continued to eat glires even after they were banned in 115 BC. The super-rich Titus Pompeius kept casks full of them in a four-mile enclosure. They fattened the dormice in terracotta containers where, according to Varro, "acorns, walnuts, or chestnuts are placed; and when a cover is placed over the jars, they grow fat in the dark." They were served roasted and dipped in honey or stuffed with pork and pine nuts. Mmmmmm!!

2. Three Squeak Mice
(Ancient to Contemporary China)

This is not for the squeamish. Still popular in the Guangdong area, so-called because a live baby mouse squeaks three times: once when you pick him up, once when you dip him in sauce (usually cold soy) and once when you bite him.

3. Ambergris
(globally, especially in 17th–19th century)

Herman Melville wrote a whole chapter about it in Moby Dick. The French epicure Jean Anthelme Brillat-Savarin recommended it with chocolate. What exactly is Ambergris? It's a fancy name for the excretions from sperm whales–there is a scholarly debate whether it's closer to vomit or faeces, but this hasn't put people off using it as a flavouring for centuries.   The sperm whale produces this substance in its intestinal tract as a protection from the sharp beaks of ingested fish. Ambergris was mostly used for perfume, but its "musky" flavour was also popular in ice-cream. Do Ben and Jerry's know?

4. Calf's Foot Jelly (Victorian Britain)

Britain has long enjoyed a global reputation for culinary excellence, and never more so when she ruled the waves. The toast sandwich was a highlight (which was a sandwich filled with, erm…toast) but the summit of Victorian cooking was Calf's Foot Jelly.

Given to people who weren't feeling very well, it probably hastened their demise. Like the toast sandwich, Calf's Foot Jelly did what it says on the tin. Take some braised beef leftover, add Madeira, sugar, spices, more leftover meat, citrus and cinnamon. Then make it into jelly and take it to an ailing relative, whose property you have a reasonable chance of inheriting.

5. Weasel (Ancient Rome)

Even with their dodgy taste buds, the Romans rarely went for cooked weasels. Elagabalus once served them on vast platters at a party but, like so many things with the teenage tyrant, it was largely for show. However, it was seen as a cure for epilepsy and snake bites, so this tasty rodent occasionally appeared on the menu.

Pliny the Elder wrote that the "brains of a weasel are also considered very good, dried and taken in drink; the liver, too, of that animal, or the testes, uterus, or paunch, dried and taken with coriander." Fortunately, there were more palatable alternatives to weasel if you were suffering from epilepsy. Some doctors recommended smoked camel's brain or beaver's testicles.

6. Cat (Medieval Europe)

Eating one of the planet's nicest creatures was perfectly acceptable during the Middle Ages, providing you chopped off its head and threw it away, because "it is not for eating, for they say that eating the brains will cause him who eats them to lose his senses and judgment." Before this, the dead cat was flayed and buried for a day and a night to improve the flavour. Apparently, baked cat was good for throat inflammation.

Medieval people–as cruel as they were stupid.

7. Singing Chicken (Medieval Europe)

We now avoid meat dishes that resemble what we're eating. It was different in the Middle Ages; they loved to see what the animal looked like. With singing chicken, they went a stage further and added sound effects. They stuffed the bird with mercury and sulphur, so it sang, or rather whistled when reheated.

8. Rôti Sans Pareil (19th century France)

Engastration is the art of stuffing one animal inside others to create a hybrid dish. The most famous modern example is the American turducken: which is a roast chicken inside a duck stuffed into a

turkey. But this is paltry (or poultry, if you must) compared to the Tudor Christmas pie.

Shaped like a coffin, it was a turkey, stuffed with a goose, chicken, partridge, wildfowl, hare and pigeon. No wonder they had to winch the ageing Henry VIII onto his horse.

But even Big Hal's yuletide snack couldn't compare with the Rôti Sans Pareil.

Invented by the French foodie, Grimod de la Reynier, the Roast Without Equal was "...a bustard stuffed with a turkey, a goose, a pheasant, a chicken, a duck, a guinea fowl, a teal, a woodcock, a partridge, a plover, a lapwing, a quail, a thrush, a lark, an ortolan bunting and a garden warbler."

9. Kiviak (Greenland)

Imagine this on Jamie Oliver's TV Special: "Christmas Dishes from Around the World." Kiviak is an Inuit winter feast. Take a few hundred sea birds and lovingly stuff them in a seal carcass. Don't bother removing anything like feathers or beaks. You must cover it in seal grease, then sew up the carcass and ferment for roughly a year. Eat raw.

10. Garbage (Medieval Europe)

Metaphorically, medieval people often ate a lot of garbage, but sometimes it was literally so. An English royal cookbook from the 14th century told chefs to "Take faire Garbage chikenes hedes, ffete, lyvers, And gysers and wassh hem clene. caste hem into a faire potte." A modern translation is: bung a load of the rubbish from a chicken in a pot. Note that they regarded this dish as suitable for kings; imagine what the peasants ate.

Let Nature Take its Course: History's Worst Medicines

In the old days, if you were ill, you would go to the wise woman of the village. Her herbs and potions had been passed down over the centuries, from generations of wise women at one with nature. Sounds great, but this was an age where life expectancy was thirty. What you got was a couple of pagan incantations and some boiled-up tree roots that at best would make you vomit violently and at worst kill you. But we can't be too smug. Despite the scientific revolution, humans were still killing each other in the name of profit well into the twentieth century.

1. Trepanning, Neolithic Times to Present

Trepanning comes from the Greek word trypanon, meaning "a borer." For that's all it is, boring holes into your skull. From the flint tools of the hunter gatherers to the modern surgical implements of today, people have been drilling into each other's heads for thousands of years.

There is some use for trepanning. They used it in certain cases to remove fragments from the skull after accidents. Archaeological evidence shows high survival rates; though without anaesthetic, having someone bore a hole into your skull doesn't bear thinking about. But mostly, it's balderdash. They generally used trepanning to get rid of evil spirits, especially if the patient was suffering from mental illness. There are still some advocates around who claim trepanning increases blood volume. In 1965, Dutchman Bart Huges used a dentist drill on his own skull for that purpose. He survived.

2. Cannibalism, Prehistory–19th Century

Humans have used cannibalism for ritualistic purposes from prehistoric times. Sometimes people on the brink of starvation have eaten other humans, like during the siege of Leningrad in World War II. However, it has also been a persistent belief that digesting other people can have medicinal purposes. The Romans believed gladiators' blood could cure epilepsy. During the Renaissance, even a sophisticated humanist like Marsilio Ficino, recommended old people should drink the blood of adolescents to revitalise them. If you were too poor to afford an apothecary, you could buy blood at a discount rate after public executions. By the seventeenth century, crushed skulls had become popular as a cure for gout and dropsy. Charles II once paid six thousand pounds (a fortune in those days) for the recipe.

3. Heroin, Mid-19th–Early 20th Century

Freud thought cocaine might be an antidote to depression. Queen Victoria enjoyed the odd tincture of opium as a relaxant, so perhaps it's not surprising that heroin was once thought potentially beneficial. It was originally created as a "safe" alternative to morphine. The world-renowned chemists, Bayer, sold it as a medicine for coughs and colds. Heroin was aimed particularly at the children's market. Bayer boasted that after taking heroin, the child's "cough disappears" along with the child, presumably. Evidence of its addictiveness did not dissuade Bayer from selling heroin for almost 20 years.

4. Radium Water, Early 20th Century

"There are men who affirm that… in fact, this yellow atom, so insignificant in appearance, eventually will prove one of the greatest boons to ailing mankind that ever was discovered."
~ **Chicago Tribune.**

The discovery of radium by Marie and Pierre Curie in 1898 excited the medical profession as a potential cure for cancer. Radium rays quickly proved its worth. However, radium was used for a variety of other illness with less beneficial effect. Radium water became a fad in the 1920s and '30s, and a whole industry grew up around it. There were radium cocktails and radium clubs, where you could hang with friends, play cards, chat and drink radiation. Many claims were made for its curative powers: it could fix diabetes, rheumatism, anaemia, arthritis, sciatica, impotence, and the confidence tricksters' old standby, reverse the ageing process. There was disquieting evidence that radium was killing people, but it took the high-profile death of a steel magnet, Eben M. Byers (who drank radium every day for two years) to jolt the US government into action. Health inspectors started prosecuting sellers, and another magic bullet was found to be nothing more than a blank.

5. Tapeworms, Early 20th Century

Probably the single most stupid cure for weight loss ever invented. You swallow a beef tapeworm cyst or a tapeworm egg. Your new friend matures inside the intestines, then starts eating much of your food. When you are happy with your weight, you take anti-parasitic pills and expel the tapeworm. Simple.

Except tapeworms can grow up to 30 feet and cause epilepsy, severe headaches and dementia. Why not just eat less junk food?

6. Snake Oil, 18th and 19th Century

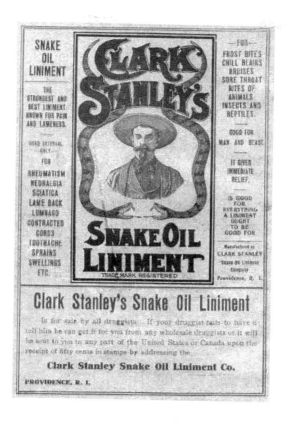

A snake oil salesman now means someone who pedals fake cures. It was introduced to the US either by the British (where viper oil was sold as a cure-all in the 18th century) or Chinese railway workers, as snake oil had long been part of Oriental medicine.

Typically, a huckster with the gift of the gab would travel round the country in a medicine show. An assistant would pretend to be an independent witness who had been "cured" by this elixir. The con men would then hotfoot it out of town before anyone realised they'd been duped.

Federal regulation of drugs was non-existent. Any claim, no matter how bogus, was perfectly legal. After the Pure Food and Drug Act (1906), the government started testing and found it contained anything but snake oil. Camphor, chilli peppers and turpentine were staple ingredients.

7. Hemiglossectomy, 17th–19th Century

This means cutting out part of a patient's tongue, still used today for sufferers of oral cancer. Fair enough. But two hundred years ago, stutters received the same treatment to prevent muscle spasms. No anaesthetic was used, and the poor stutterers sometimes died from loss of blood. Many who survived became mute without the control of their tongues.

8. The Skull Cure, 1500-500 BCE

Babylonians had a cure for someone who ground their teeth at night. The reason for the grinding was that the ghosts of dead relatives were visiting you. The solution? Sleep with a human skull next to you for a week. This would ward away the spirit of your dead grandad–but only if you roused yourself seven times in the night and licked the skull.

9. Goats Testicles, Early 20th Century

"He should be considered a charlatan and a quack in the ordinary, well-understood meaning of those words."
~ The jury in a libel trial John Brinkley lost.

John Brinkley was a fake doctor who made a fortune but was eventually exposed as a fraud. Brinkley claimed he could cure impotence and restore fertility by implanting goats' testicles into men's scrotums. The cure didn't work, and many patients died. This did not seem to harm Brinkley's popularity, and he almost won the governorship of Kansas. When regulations were tightened and the American Medical Association tried to shut him down, he moved to Mexico to broadcast his quackery out of reach of US broadcasting law. Eventually he died penniless from many lawsuits, often from angry customers who didn't lack the cojones to take him to court.

10. Urine Baths, Middle Ages

Urine was seen as efficacious against the plague. Doctors recommended soaking in a tub of urine several times a day. A drink or two of the golden vintage before bedtime wouldn't hurt either.

ABOUT THE AUTHOR

Adam Powell studied History at Newcastle University and has taught the subject for over twenty years in international schools. He originally trained as a journalist and worked for a range of publications, writing satirical pieces for *The Voice of Reason, Deadbrain and Humorfeed* and *The Sabotage Times*. He was also included in the *People of Few Words* humour anthology. He is married to the children's author, Carmen Powell, and has one daughter.

In 2019, his book about World War 1 veterans, *Soldiering On*, was published.

Recommended Websites

http://youtu.be/I0VSVQonb9g

http://horrible-histories.co.uk/

http://www.madmonarchs.nl/

http://history.inrebus.com/

http://www.cracked.com/humor-history.html

http://www.funny-english-errors.com/fun/erwins-essays.html

http://www.leo.org/information/freizeit/fun/history.html

http://coolmaterial.com/roundup/if-historical-events-had-facebook-statuses/

http://www.snopes.com/history/history.asp

.

Made in the USA
San Bernardino, CA
29 June 2020

73888352R00124